Are you suffering from cystitis?

Its symptoms can be: a constant urge to urinate long after the bladder has been emptied, sharp spears of pain in the area, and blood in the urine. Urinary and vaginal problems torment millions of women, but the illness is still treated lightly by the medical profession, and many women are embarrassed to discuss the matter with their physician. In addition to the pain they suffer, the fear of recurrence may inhibit sexual relationships.

Angela Kilmartin has gathered testimony from women of all ages along with medical and physiological facts to help you understand the reasons for your infections, cope with them when they happen and, best of all, keep them from recurring. By taking care of your health yourself, you can have a cystitis-free life—and a more enjoyable one.

"Informative . . . important and comprehensive."
—*Bestways* magazine

"This candid, informative volume does a service to the many women who suffer from chronic attacks of cystitis."
—*Publishers Weekly*

"A fine handbook for women confronting the disease."
—*Chattanooga Daily Times*

CYSTITIS

The Complete
Self-Help Guide

Angela Kilmartin

Foreword by Robert S. Mendelsohn, M.D.

WARNER BOOKS

A Warner Communications Company

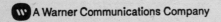

For
You and Rowena

Preface

You're probably reading this because your life has been damaged, as mine was, by cystitis. Let me reassure you at once—you need never suffer another cystitis attack again. I'll show you how to analyze your life to learn what is causing your cystitis, and what you should do about it. Avoiding cystitis is quite simple, once you know how. But it took me a long while to find out.

When people ask me how long I worked on the research for this book, I always think of my wedding—a simple white ceremony in a medieval English church—and the subsequent honeymoon. From that lovely moment on, for the next five years, my life was a deep well of pain and frustration caused by recurrent cystitis and yeast infections.

Finally I was given the first clue to self-help, and my life started to change for the better. As I learned more, I became something of a crusader. Determined never to let another woman suffer unnecessarily, I pioneered self-help in conjunction with modern medicine, wrote a book and pamphlets on cystitis, lectured, appeared on TV, made a film—and successfully pressured the British government for leaflets. I've also given birth to two beautiful

children and kept my marriage together, which sometimes seems like the greatest feat of all.

I've stopped my own cystitis attacks, and helped
countless women stop theirs. This book will help you stop
yours. Forever.

—Angela Kilmartin

Foreword

I have never met Angela Kilmartin, but now I can't wait for the chance. Reading this book really disturbed me, as it will most physicians. I kept thinking, "Why didn't I ever learn this in medical school?" And I couldn't help speculating on the state of medical practice that leads a former fashion model to find out more about cystitis than M.D.'s know.

Cystitis, UTI (urinary tract infection), and NSU (non-specific urethritis) are subjects usually covered in one too-short forty-minute lecture in medical school, if that. So when I meet Mrs. Kilmartin, I intend to congratulate her on writing this book. I want to argue with her on some issues (for example, implying that tonsillectomy may improve urinary infections), but I want to thank her for teaching me much that I didn't know (e.g., don't use the launderette for washing underwear).

And I want to discuss with her various strategies for marketing this book. Perhaps it should be introduced into the OB course entitled "How Obstetric Intervention Causes Cystitis," with Mrs. Kilmartin as the lecturer. Certainly it should be prominently featured in all pharmacies, so that a patient can read about the prescription before deciding to have it filled.

You may find that this book somewhat shakes your faith in your physician. If so, good. That's what the self-help consumer movement in medicine is about—taking on the responsibility for your own health. And you will learn how to analyze your life to find out what's causing your cystitis attacks, which is the first step toward preventing them. But if you want the best of all possible worlds, buy a second copy and give it to your doctor!

Robert S. Mendelsohn, M.D.,
author of *Confessions of a
Medical Heretic*

Acknowledgments

I am quite sure that the reader never understands that this page is one of the more difficult ones for any author to compile. Just where do I stop since obviously so many people are part of any book's history? This time I have decided to broaden my horizons and include people indirectly associated with my book as well as those directly concerned. There is no order of selection, just most grateful and lasting thanks to everyone mentioned.

Cynthia Clarke
Mr. and Mrs. A. Creasey
B. Gittelson
Mr. and Mrs. Michael Ker-Davies
Paul, Rowena, and Rory Kilmartin
Mrs. E. Kinnear
Mr. and Mrs. F. W. Mendham
Christina Murphy
Hans and Dagmar Pelzer
S. Schreibman
Warner Books and their internal sufferers
Yellow Pages directory of Manhattan

Contents

CYSTITIS

1. Cystitis and Associated Conditions

This miserable and distressing women's illness has gone unnoticed, unresearched, and uncared about for too long. The lack of helpful medical aid has caused social, physical, and mental distress of a torturous kind to women in every street in every town, in every city, and in every country. Proof of this comes all too easily. No country, government, or health department bothers to keep figures of its incidence. No doctor or hospital bothers to keep a weekly, monthly, or yearly record either. Only a urology department engaged on a strict limited numbers research program holds any indication at all of the symptoms and sufferings which go on in any group of cystitis patients.

Why are there no figures? There is a simple reason. The numbers of cases of cystitis or bladder conditions are so great that they are as common as the common cold and winter chest. Not worth noting, not worth checks on a piece of paper, not worth employing a few health officers for a year to find out how much cystitis costs a nation in drugs alone, not worth bothering about because it's one of those things women have to learn to live with, not worth bothering about because you don't die of it! Here is a random case history; there are millions such:

"In my case cystitis first reared its ugly head nine years ago on my honeymoon. My doctor said that I had honeymoon cystitis and would grow out of it, but after several months of more attacks it became obvious I was not going to grow out of it. After four years and dozens of attacks I was free of it during my first pregnancy, but once intercourse was resumed the cystitis seemed more virulent than ever. My doctor at that time neglected to carry out routine urine tests, so the treatment was guesswork. For another year I put up with it, and when a much-needed holiday went to ruin from more cystitis, I became extremely depressed and developed a stomach ulcer from the worry. They put me on barbiturates for the depression, but I developed suicidal tendencies and one day threw all the pills down the toilet— either that or take the lot. Again we sought urological help, and a dilatation was recommended. This was done on the spot with no local anesthetic, which was absolute hell. I had to drive a long way home on my own and felt very embarrassed at the pain and the way I'd cried. Over the months I became frigid and frightened, and my marriage suffered dreadfully. Doctors do not seem to be aware of the problems which come with recurrent attacks of cystitis. I ended up having psychiatric treatment for the frigidity, which helped a lot since the psychiatrist was a woman and highly sympathetic, but the cystitis didn't go away. At the moment I am attending yet another hospital for treatment, but the doctors aren't really interested. Because you don't die from it, they suggest that it's just one of those things you have to live with. Is this the future that women sufferers from cystitis are doomed to endure or is the medical profession as a whole going to do something definite to give us the help we need so badly?"

A challenging cry. What defense can be put forward by doctors?

"I appreciate that many female cystitis patients may feel very critical of doctors at times, but they should remember that we, the doctors, are only repeating the ghastly teaching received from teaching hospitals over the past thirty years on this subject, and it isn't improving as fast as it might even now. Sooner or later patients and doctors will have to get together on this subject if only because of the sheer abundance of cystitis, which is quite beyond the capacity of the doctors to deal with."

An honest and, in its way, a constructive reply. If indeed poor teaching is the reason behind the improper medical care at present, then we suspect that it must be true because of its daily practical exposure to failure in consulting rooms the world over. Young doctors are still as bad as, if not worse than, the older ones. The older ones do in the course of a lifetime in medicine pick up some facts more useful than the bland statements of their professors. But younger doctors, full of their newly acquired importance, scorn any suggestion that their training may have been incomplete on the everyday subject of urinary tract troubles.

Urinary tract infection is still given only a half day's worth of lectures in a five-year training course at a teaching hospital.

Yet the average family doctor can support a claim that 10 percent of all consultations are solely for cystitis. That doesn't include all the dozens of associated conditions like prolapsed uterus or yeast*—just bladder infections and inflammations which are lumped together for ease under the word "cystitis."

Medical students leave their training with the following information on what to do with a woman suffering from attacks of cystitis:

1. Test her urine for bacteria (germs). It's called an MSU (Mid Stream Urine).

2. Give her a ten-day course of antibiotics either before or after the result of the MSU.

3. Send her for a kidney X ray.

4. Send her for an exploratory bladder operation called a cystoscopy.

5. Prescribe more antibiotics of all sorts.

And that's it basically. If the patient makes a fuss, she might be fobbed off with a dilatation to make the urethra bigger or a cautery, which involves burning away the inflamed urethral skin. (The urethra is the tiny tube leading from the bladder to the outside.)

So if the teaching side of our medical institutions has nothing more to offer in fifty years of research to its future doctors, we can hardly blame the doctors. They're not told that it won't work until they experience the failure rate in the big wide world. Research, in truth, has been steady. Drug firms know that by finding a curative drug, they'll add to the profits already being raked in by recurrent prescriptions for recurrent cystitis. Each antibiotic advertised in medical and pharmaceutical magazines claims another 10 percent increase in

---

*Also known as moniliasis, candidiasis, thrush, or fungus. For convenience, I'm going to call it yeast.

success over its neighbors. Whole- and half-page ads in such magazines appear in every main language all over the world. It's a common and profitable illness all right! The manufacturers of antibiotics spend an undisclosed but large amount of money every year on making sure their products stay before the doctor's eyes. Much money is spent on drug research, since investment yields high returns.

Medical research is done almost solely within the departments of urology. Animals are infected with bacteria; machines are devised to measure urine flow and force of flow; symposia are held to listen to some professor from another continent lecture on his favorite new technique for cutting the bladder neck or such like. The search is always on for THE CURE—the one and only, the ultimate answer to recurrent cystitis.

The trouble is, they can't seem to find it. There's a reason why they can't. The one and only cure never will exist! If that depresses you, reader, it shouldn't; it should make you jump for joy because, at last, a new door is about to open for you. Although the tried-and-tested door of searching for a cure has always failed to open, it can now remain happily closed. There is no secret cure beyond it. The new door will certainly open, and through it you and your doctors are going to learn and triumph over your cystitis.

That new door has a sign on it which says:

SELF-HELP

We in this modern world have forgotten the skills of our forebears. We have forgotten or never learned how great-grandmama dealt with her bodily ills. She and generations before her had no nurse or gynecologist to examine her vagina or uterus. The only time that such qualified staff used to approach was during labor, and then the patient was often swathed in sheets and nightdress. There was no interest in women's bladders because the women were too embarrassed ever to mention such problems and indeed because they didn't have as many such problems as our generation does.

Great-grandmama didn't have antibiotics. She had suffusions of local herbs in boiling water. Camomile tea was widely used, along with mint and parsley. All, when drunk in quantities, with perhaps some belladonna for pain relief, would have a beneficial effect on urinary trouble. Minds were simple in medical thought and medical deed. If your urine burned, then as with all things burning, water, lots of it, could quench the fire. Such simplicity may well have applied to passing urine. If it burned, then water it down. Not only did the water come down, but it also came out, our renal organs being as they are, and with the flowing urine came the germs. Thus, to deal with infections the concerned organs were encouraged to help expel their own illnesses.

Something else that didn't bother ladies of old as it does today is frequency of intercourse. Again and simply, men and women wore far more clothes than we do. It took a long while to become bodily available. If your desire overcame such difficult trivia, you next had social pressures. Working-class women in rows of cottages or tenements had upwards of ten children milling around and neighbors always popping in. Middle and upper classes had servants prowling around and rigid daily social etiquettes to observe. So daytime intercourse was practically unheard of except in the field behind the hedgerow!

Nighttime brought a certain amount of relief; but clothing was still an obstacle, and so was warmth. The old adage of lying there and taking it was as much to get it over with quickly for fear of being cold as for male relief. Bouncing around on a bed with a guttering fire and layers of woollies on to keep warm isn't exactly erotic. So without contraceptives sex frequently was only of the baby-making kind, and when great-grandmama discovered eventually how babies were made and she didn't want a thirteenth, she moved bedrooms.

Of course, her span of life was less than that of women today. She was a drudge and a machine for baby bearing. When man wrote the inevitable end to the marriage vows "till death do us part," he knew that might mean only nine months and multiples of nine months. Women frequently died in childbirth. If they surmounted that regular hazard, they wore themselves out in the process anyway. Today in the Third World women still expect to live for only forty-five or fifty years. They seldom reach or understand menopause, yet emancipated women now have this added difficulty of health in later life.

"Sooner or later patients and doctors will have to get together on this subject if only because of the sheer abundance of cystitis, which is quite beyond the capacity of the doctors to deal with"—Doctor.

Here is the honest admission that despite all research, the medical profession is at a loss to know what next to do. Whatever else you may think of your doctor, he is not a masochist. He would much rather you got better and stopped pestering him. He is fed up to the teeth with your frequent visits and cries for help. He gets cross and rude out of sheer embarrassment and failure.

"There's nothing more I can do for you; you'll have to learn to live with it."

And if he really has sent you for all the available tests and prescribed all the available pills, what more can you expect him to do? He's not Christ; he can't work a personal miracle for you. He can suggest a faith healer, but the chances of that working are nil.

No, no! The time has come for you to rethink your body, your health. The time has come for you to do something about yourself and stop expecting the man in the white coat to reach for his prescription pad and more pills. If great-grandmama managed, so can you—with some help.

Women have been turning of late to self-help mostly because of inadequate medical help in gynecology and obstetrics. But there's another reason. Many young women leave home early and never get to learn what mother learned from her mother. The rift between old and young women is widening. Our sexual freedom makes for conversational reticence, and the last thing we would dream of doing is asking mother what to do if your vagina hurts and stings after intercourse. But before the advent of books it was only word of mouth that helped young women through early sexual encounters.

Talk to a woman of seventy or eighty in a chatty mood, and you can learn something as important as this:

> "On my street years ago the street was your life. You lived on the stoop, and the world was there. A confinement in process would have all the women congregating to exchange tales of confinements, happinesses, and sorrows. Not only did a marriage set eyelids winking, but everyone knew in that close

comradeship that the girl was walking around for three months with no panties on."

Now why? And who told her about this? It was street folklore; she just knew it. As you will learn later on in this book, the girl could do nothing better than walk around without panties during this period of sexual adjustment. But we who know it all immediately pull on our gorgeous lacy nylon bikini briefs and pour ourselves into erotically tight trousers or jeans almost immediately after withdrawal.

You cannot expect your doctor to tell you not to wear panties after intercourse. It's not his job to take the place of older women. It is his job to spend time with seriously sick people, and you are not seriously sick. But since the last three generations of women have neglected their own health and that of their daughters, it's going to take a book to retell the rules and regulations governing prevention and management of cystitis and associated conditions.

In 1972 my first book for patients about cystitis was written and named *Understanding Cystitis*. It had only one chapter on self-help. This new book is entirely self-help, and by use of the medically approved guidelines offered here it is possible for the recurrent cystitis and vaginitis sufferer to eliminate all or most of her symptoms. This book holds more information on these subjects than has ever been collated and put into print before. Read it slowly, carefully, and with much thought. Keep it by you for reference always, and never be dismayed by an out-of-the-blue recurrence of your trouble. There is always a *reason*, and when you know that, you will search with cheerfulness through this book for ideas.

If you suffer from cystitis at intervals, you will never go through the rest of your life entirely free of it. As with vaginitis, you must adhere to the rules of prevention all your life and be ready to laugh when you let yourself down, or when your age lets you down, for stages of life, as well as triggers like alcohol, will make you more susceptible to urinary troubles. Many women go trouble-free until fifty years old, others till seventy years; still others unfortunately start at thirteen years and younger. It is certainly a female complaint, and we do have to learn to live with it.

2. Cystitis
in Modern Times

The word "cystitis" is a combination of *cyst*—a Greek word for a hollow pouch, sac, or bladder—and *itis*—an inflammation. Today we think in terms of cysts as pus-filled sacs similar to boils, and the association with bladder is perhaps a little too ancient now to be really meaningful. Certainly doctors use the word "cystitis" haphazardly, lumping together all sorts of bladder troubles under its title. However, more and more we are told, particularly in venereology, of urethritis, and when there is no significant amount of germs, it is called nonspecific urethritis.

Separation and distinction of these terms are important. A bladder infection feels different from a urethral infection. Urethral pain in the male feels "thin," lengthy, and takes a while to become the heavier bladder pain. The shorter female urethra also has a "thin" feeling of pain, but this develops faster into bladder pain. These two diagrams show how:

Side view of male renal system

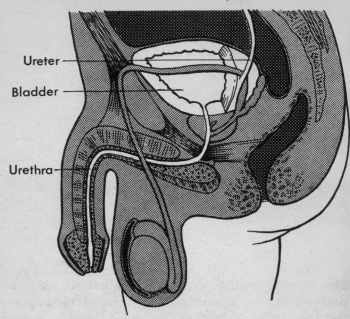

Ureter

Bladder

Urethra

Side view of female renal system

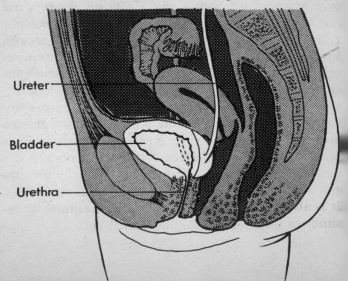

Ureter

Bladder

Urethra

True cystitis has three symptoms:

1. Pain when one passes urine
2. Frequency of passing urine
3. Sometimes blood loss from the urethra when urine is passed.

Ascending "feelings," "prickings," "knifelike pain," "sensations" are the commonest ways of complaining about symptoms to a doctor, but it can take only an hour or so for these feelings to reach the bladder. In a short time the bladder wall becomes involved, and heavier pain in the lower abdomen shows that a form of cystitis is now *in situ*. Progression up the ureters and toward the kidneys brings a dull ache in the back and almost always a temperature and malaise.

This is classic renal pyelitis and may be dangerous. Bacteria reaching the kidneys and remaining unchecked could cause scarring and minute diminution of kidney function. Renal pyelitis must be avoided and treated. Too many patients on kidney machines are there because kidney infection has gone unchecked.

Urethritis—inflammation of the urethra—is the point at which prevention and self-help are incredibly important. At this time it is possible to prevent ascension of germs or inflammatory substances from doing damage to the bladder and kidneys. At this time speed and instant routine are more important than going to the doctor. If you leave the sensations alone, you will end up in a far worse state, having to have lengthy medical intervention.

First aid at the start of these sensations is patient-controlled, patient-worked, patient-achieved. It is always safer to begin at the first twinge or instinct of impending trouble than it is to "wait and

see if it will go away by itself." It won't and will
worsen instead.

Worsening means increasing pain in the urethra, frequent visits to the toilet to the point where
you daren't get up from the seat, and even smears of
blood on the toilet paper. The more attacks occur,
the quicker the bleeding stage is reached because
scars in the urethra from previous attacks will just
open up again. This pain, particularly during the
passage of urine down the little urethral tube, is not
simply "burning glass" but is often like a minor operation without anesthetic. In fact, each trickle of
hot acid urine on the scarred and broken skin is ut-
ter agony. What is worse is that you cannot bathe it
or soothe it as you can an external cut. You can't
touch it at all. So distinctive is it that many women
fail to try a simple painkilling drug—the pain is just
too violent. One woman wrote me:

> "In your television program you showed a short
> film of a woman getting up in the night to deal with
> an attack of cystitis, and that depicted the loneliness
> and utter isolation one feels at these times. When
> husband is asleep, oblivious to what is really going
> on, oblivious to the misery and the depression his
> wife is feeling, it is these midnight attacks which are
> so soul-destroying."

If you don't employ immediate first aid, the
chances are that you will be too distressed and too ill
even to get to your doctor, and these days he certainly won't come to you. Then you must rely on
your family or friends to get drugs from the doctor
as soon as his office opens, and by that time you'll be
well advanced into the ascending progression of cystitis.

What will the doctor prescribe? Antibiotics or sulfonamides or even an old-fashioned bottle of green potassium citrate?

All these compounds can cause side effects. Potassium citrate is difficult to hold down because it tastes foul, and after you have thrown up a few spoonfuls, it's obvious that the bladder and urethra cannot be touched by it. Some people do take it, of course, and it can be helpful, though the small dosages every few hours make time go by very slowly when you're crying in pain.

Sulfonamides are older than antibiotics. Gantrisin, Bactrim, Furadantin, and Nitrofurantoin are the best known but have nausea and vomiting as distressing side effects. Some women find this diminishes if the tablets are taken at mealtimes, but it doesn't always work. Skin rashes are another side effect, but at least these drugs are safe during the greater part of pregnancy.

Antibiotics are the commonest way of dealing with bladder troubles. Fortunately many doctors are not prescribing them in quite the prolonged dosages which they once did. A dosage of five days now is normal, and this is tolerable; but their action in your body can last up to six weeks before the natural body cells return to full health. The action of antibiotics is to remove bacteria—*all* bacteria, not just the bad, but also the good. This means that your cells have to reestablish their normal constituents somehow, and a good supply of vitamins helps greatly. On a prolonged course of antibiotics lasting several weeks (which the medical profession is still fond of prescribing in cases of recurrent cystitis), the patient feels washed out and lethargic and finds it immensely difficult to get out of bed.

An even more insidious side effect of antibiotics is yeast, which you may know as moniliasis, candidiasis, or vaginal thrush. It is a fungus which comes first in the fight for possession of those vacated cells after the course of antibiotics. It goes in for warm, moist places, such as the tongue, mouth, vagina, intestines, and rectum. (Men get moniliasis, too, in the mouth, intestines, and rectum.) Vaginitis takes the form of a creamy liquid discharge which emerges from the vagina out along the perineum (the best word yet for that area which contains all of your body's private openings). Out there in that warm, moist area vaginitis spreads around and soon finds

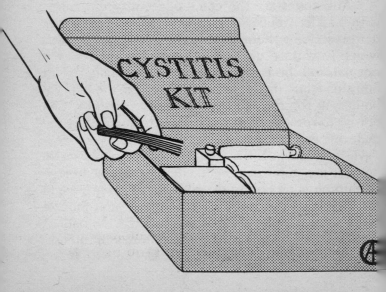

its way into the urethra. It irritates the old urethral scars, and they open up again, giving what seems like another attack of cystitis. So back you go to the doctor, and he, often without a perineal examination, prescribes yet another course of antibiotics!

Although I'm stressing the side effects of these drugs, they are, in an advanced stage of cystitis and pyelitis, unfortunately necessary. The trouble with urinary bacteria is that any number of different ones produce the same symptoms. Unless you know that three or more attacks have been microscopically diagnosed as a specific infection like *E. coli,* you should have your urine put as quickly as possible under a microscope for detection. But if you do know for sure that you have a recurrent *E. coli* infection, that is uncomplicated and doesn't, in its early stages, need medical intervention.

Whatever the type of germ, though, the following first aid is applicable and in truth can be helpful for further diagnosis.

1. Always keep a sterile small screw-top jar for a sample of your urine. Wash your hands first and then clean your perineum front to back with a couple of cotton balls and warm water. Pass some urine into the toilet bowl, and then allow a small amount of urine to flow directly into a sterile measuring cup or bowl—one with a lip for pouring is easiest. Finish your flow in the toilet, and transfer your captured urine to the small jar.

If you are doing this in a clinic, the sample will go under a microscope immediately, but if you do it at home, you should store it in the refrigerator until you can get it to the lab.

2. Wash your hands, and again swab the entrance to the urethra with a cotton ball, front to back.

3. Now start the basic work of alleviating pain, preventing ascension of the infection, and emptying the bladder. Your bladder is like a toilet bowl—its contents can be flushed away, and our urinary mechanisms provide for just this. If your bladder nerve endings are given an impulse to empty, by a strong acidic urine or an infection, they will tell you to go to the toilet. Counteracting these impulses means that you are going to fill your bladder with liquid until the urine runs out colorless for three hours. Colorless urine doesn't hurt and doesn't harbor infection. Dark urine or infected urine stings badly.

On the first sensations of an impending attack start to drink. Drink water-based liquids, i.e., flavored only; no concentrates of any kind. First you will drink a pint of water, hot or cold, mixed with a teaspoonful of sodium bicarbonate. Every twenty minutes for the next three hours you will drink a half pint of water, flavored either as a weak tea, diluted fruit soda (*not* juice!), or just ordinary cold water. Within thirty to forty minutes you should begin to go to the toilet frequently, and although the first couple of times may sting, this will go away as more and more water arrives in the bladder.

Bicarbonate of soda is an alkalinizing agent and will help stop the urine from burning. American doctors recommend the imbibing of cranberry juice during an attack. Obviously they've never tried passing pure acid! Although it may well take away the breeding conditions necessary for germs to thrive inside the bladder, it will certainly reduce the patient to a screaming pitch. With bicarbonate and water you can be in tolerable comfort while you still expel and reduce the bacterial content of your bladder.

So remember—one half-pint liquid every twenty minutes for three hours; then decrease this slowly if you wish.

4. The teaspoonful of bicarbonate must be repeated. Doctors have described one teaspoonful an hour for three or four hours as being perfectly acceptable and without any side effects. (Anyone with blood pressure problems or heart conditions must discuss this process with the family physician first.) Some women prefer the potassium citrate or even mixing the teaspoon of bicarbonate with jam. Choose the method you prefer and find easiest to take.

5. Comfort. Well, have you personally ever thought of taking a painkiller? Many women don't, but in an attack two or three painkillers, such as the Extra Strength Tylenol, will prove very relaxing and provide a reduction in the pain level.

Now there are three pain reducers at work—water, bicarbonate, and analgesic. That must make you feel happier.

6. With all this action going, you need a place to put your feet up if possible. Bed is best, but a comfortable chair would be all right. If you're in an office, find a soft cushion to put on your chair. Explain to those around you what you're doing; it will prevent raised eyebrows and sniggering remarks. If you tell people what the problem is, you will receive all help, support, and attention. Don't worry about the frequent visits to the toilet—it's all very essential and scientific. If you're in a hotel bedroom where you don't like or don't trust the tap water, phone down for bottled water—but order it all at one time so that the inquisitive staff doesn't become awkward. You may need six large bottles, perhaps more.

7. Something nice and hot is delightfully comforting to press against your stomach or back. Some women have two hot-water bottles at such times, one for the back and a cooler or well-wrapped one to sit on. There's a technique to this. Squat or lie so that the knees are drawn up and you can part your genital lips (labia). Position the bottle carefully between the labia so that the urethral and vaginal openings have the heat directly on them. The temperature of the bottle must not be hot enough to burn you, of course, but the purpose is to make the skin around the urethral opening hotter than the urine. When you go to the bathroom again, the urine feels cooler because the skin is hotter. Try it; it's such a relief for the urine not to feel as though it's burning.

8. All this water intake is no good unless you are also steadily voiding it. Usually the sensations or pain will keep the bladder stimulated, but sometimes they don't. In such cases a diuretic pill is useful; but these have to be prescribed, and not all doctors would do so in this particular case. Our homes contain diuretics, however. Strong black coffee once an hour can help the bladder to work, but under no other circumstances should cystitis or kidney patients drink coffee. A cup of strong tea can also have a diuretic effect, but do *not* use alcohol during this management process. Ask your local health food store for a good diuretic product, and persevere until you find one that suits you personally.

9. As a final point, don't forget to swab the urethral area with warm, moist cotton balls after each visit to the toilet. You'll never make the perineum sterile, but you can certainly reduce the level of contamination from outflowing germs.

Apart from reducing an attack of cystitis and in countless cases finishing it completely, this self-help management process becomes a pointer for your doctor's efforts to find the cause of the attack. That's where the urine sample you took at the beginning of the attack comes in.

E. coli bacteria usually—in fact, almost always when caught early—are eliminated in the deluge of liquid, and no further treatment is necessary. What of other bacteria, though? A streptococcal infection will diminish but not necessarily die, and while your urine specimen is being examined, you, at home, can also feel that your urethra is still "involved" despite the three-hour management process. Antibiotics, short but sharp in dosage, would be needed when the urine culture result comes through. By maintaining a steady intake of liquid during the two and a half days of the culture growth, you can remain comfortable, and your doctor can ultimately give you the correct antibiotic to which your germs are found to be sensitive.

Suppose the urine culture comes through with "no significant bacteria"—in other words, no germs to be found. You, however, still know your urethra is involved. What do you do then?

You ask—or insist if you have to—for a vaginal checkup. Three swabs will be taken and put immediately under a microscope. The chances are that they will disclose a discharge. This will account for the incomplete help experienced after the management process. Until the discharge is dealt with, your urethra will remain involved and signaling.

Another group of women will shout that this is all very well, but they have continuous cystitis, and nothing in the way of bacteria ever shows up in cultures or vaginal swabs. First, what this group has is not true cystitis as previously spelled out. Second, the exact accuracy of MSU urine results is a bone of medical contention. Unless you are in a clinic and your urine is examined immediately under a microscope, that small sterile jar has a long wait before it is given laboratory attention. If you take your specimen at 3:00 in the morning, bring it to your doctor at 11:00 A.M., and he sends it on to a lab that afternoon, the chances of bacterial survival are limited. There is no food of the kind bacteria like in a small jar of urine, so they die and become undetectable. In borderline cases, where there isn't necessarily a good supply of pus cells but only the original bacteria which might be dead or in small numbers, out comes the culture result of "negative" or "no significant bacteria." At 3:00 in the morning the results might have been different.

By-the-textbook medicine insists that medical treatment for an attack of cystitis should not commence until the bacteria are identified and the correct drug selected. This means, theoretically, that the patient is left without help for two and a half days during the culture growth. The outcome is horrific. Halfway through the first day, infection has reached the kidneys, and the patient is racked with pain. A high temperature—103 or 104 degrees—is possible, and fever renders the patient almost insensible. Blood carries the bacteria all around the body, and they multiply as they travel. The kidneys are in danger of permanent scarring, and the entire illness can mean bed and rest for two or three weeks.

In a recent postgraduate lecture on urinary infections 100 percent of the family doctors present admitted that they did not and could not treat cystitis by the book. One man said, "I cannot send her away in what is obviously painful distress without medical treatment and help. I am sure I speak for all my colleagues here and find it easier to say it because there happen to be no bacteriologists or urologists in this lecture hall!"

Heads nodded assent, but not in triumph, for the doctors knew only too well that they were practicing hit-or-miss medicine and giving only temporary relief.

With the validity of culture growths of urine in doubt and demanding patients, the doctors all preferred to write out haphazard prescriptions for antibiotics. They felt that their reasons for so doing came in this order of importance:

1. Compassion
2. Lack of MSU validity
3. Time (prescriptions are quicker than questions)
4. Assurance of eventual relief of symptoms
5. Doctor/patient cordiality.

The self-help management process relieves the doctors of their dilemma and allows humane by-the-textbook medicine.

1. It stops the pain and distress during the wait for the culture result.
2. It stops "blind" exposure to hit-or-miss antibiotics.
3. It prevents renal scarring.
4. It prevents pyelitis and fever.
5. It prevents side effects from arising.
6. It promotes normal social life for the patient.

If the patient commences an attack at an inopportune time, such as a weekend or in the early morning, the difference between existing medical treatment and the self-help management process can be compared on this chart.

ANTIBIOTICS	SELF-HELP MANAGEMENT PROCESS
Patient has to wait for doctor's office and drugstores to open.	She starts immediate help.
has to wait for urine culture result two and a half days.	She has no wait.
has then to wait thirty-six hours for antibiotic effect.	She has no wait.
Patient thus waits a total of four to five days for relief of pain.	Three to four hours.
"Blind" antibiotics therapy is still thirty-six hours to wait for relief of pain.	Again three to four hours.
As a result of lost hours, there follow:	
A risk of pyelitis	No risk
Acute pain	Minimal pain
Hematuria (bleeding from urethra)	No hematuria
Off work one to three weeks	Work possible after four hours
Costly drugs	One box of bicarbonate of soda
Side effects:	
Possible yeast infection	No risk
Nausea	No risk
Diarrhea	No risk
Depression	Confidence
Possible immunity to antibiotics.	No immunity

Antibiotic therapy and the self-help management process are first aid. They will deal with *only that one attack,* so we all must clearly understand that more attacks may be expected in the future until the reason or cause for the cystitis is finally known. Some women get only one attack in their entire lives, and the above treatments never have to be undertaken again. But an inestimable number of patients will suffer recurrent attacks—a couple of times a year or, sadly, once a month or so.

It is these women who need the help of this book.

3. Achieving a Diagnosis

Eliminate all thoughts of *cure* from your mind. There isn't a cure and never will be because cystitis is only a symptom. What you have to do first of all is think—for yourself and for your doctor—of what might be causing your recurrent attacks. The obvious and, oddly enough, easiest question for women to answer clearly is: When did the attacks first start?

Usually an answer relates to age and to an event. It can fall in one of seven sections in the female life cycle:

- During childhood
- During puberty
- At the onset of regular sexual intercourse
- During pregnancy
- After childbirth
- During menopause
- After a hysterectomy

The seven ages of man become the seven ages of woman! More often than not urinary troubles can be related, after thought, to one of those times, but it doesn't always follow. In searching for your cause or causes of attacks, volunteer only your *own* facts for consideration. What happened to your neighbor and friend will not be what has happened to you. One reason why medical investigations so often come to a dead end is that the doctors try to push each woman with cystitis into a niche of medical rules. If your troubles don't fit the niche, or if their tests keep coming up negative, they cannot understand it at all and have no interest or time to allow your body to create its own special set of symptoms and circumstances.

In each of the seven ages of woman there is a place for medical treatment and a place for self-help. Medical diagnosis is always essential, but receiving the correct help from the variety of relevant departments is not so easy.

Once it is established that you're subject to recurrent attacks, the medical way of doing things is to refer you to a urologist. He is in charge of your renal organs and wishes to subject you to a few uncomplicated tests. His investigation is of major importance—you can live with one kidney, but you cannot live without any at all!

He will want to check your urine, and unfortunately for you the day of the long-awaited appointment finds you either with your period or in perfect urinary health between attacks. (Much discussion has been held in Great Britain as to whether urology departments should become "open"—in other words, whether a patient in full throes or starting cystitis should simply be able to walk right in. They compromise by using such a system during research programs when the guinea-pig women are given pass cards allowing immediate access day or night.)

So, after passing a beautifully clear and non-odious MSU into the nurse's special receptacle, you gloomily wait for clearance into the X ray department. Begowned in a stiff white hospital robe showing a delicate line of floppy flesh at the back where the ties don't close properly, you are invited to lie down on the X ray couch. The radiographer approaches with a large amount of blue liquid which he intends to inject into your bloodstream through a prominent vein. He should mention that as the dye passes along, it will make your arms and legs and muscles feel tingly. There is no pain whatsoever. This dye very quickly reaches your two kidneys, and on his screen the radiographer can watch its progress. It is like a barium meal traversing the stomach for a stomach X ray. The blue dye shows up the geography of your kidneys and ureters. Watching most attentively, the specialist notes any unusual twists or turns, thickenings or obstacles in the wake of the dye.

A micturating cystogram test could also have been requested by the urologist. If so, you are asked to pass water into a bowl. Again the radiographer watches intently as the ureters fill the bladder and the blue urine begins to flow into the little urethra. All this is termed IVP, short for intra (into) venous (the vein) pyelogram (kidney examination).

If you are a recurrent sufferer and have never been given an IVP, *demand* one. I recently heard of a disgraceful case involving a woman whose cystitis began when she was a child and had continued through the next twenty-five years; her mother and grandmother both had cystitis histories as well—and not one of these women had ever been given kidney X rays.

If your urine tests are negative and your IVP is also negative, gloom descends upon you. You were really hoping something would be found, as was your family doctor. Now he knows he can expect to give you supportive antibiotic therapy *ad infinitum*. Eventually, of course, you create a scene and demand further help. He now tries another investigation process called cystoscopy. One woman described her experience with this as follows:

> "I cannot bear the thought of an anesthetic because it is difficult to distinguish between sleep imposed on me by others and death. So, when I received a letter from the hospital stating that I would require a general anesthetic for this operation, I panicked. I spoke to my specialist, who insisted that there was no need for a general anesthetic and that a local one would be sufficient if I didn't mind having my legs up in the air in front of him and a couple of nurses. After more than a year of gynecological examinations, embarrassment was the least of my worries. However, when I next visited my doctor, her partner (a man) was shocked that I was to undergo a cystoscopy in full consciousness and told me I would find it a rather horrifying experience. This set me worrying again, but next time I met my own doctor (a woman). She assured me that the procedure was a minor one and there was no need for a general anesthetic.
>
> "I spent a night in hospital preceding the cystoscopy, and on inquiring what method would be used to administer the local anesthetic, I was told by a nurse that it would be a rather painful injection around the urethral area. My grounds for alarm were increased when just outside the operating

room the nurse tried to persuade me to 'just have a whiff of the gas' as the 'operation' would certainly be painful. I thanked her for her advice but refused and went into the operating room feeling like a patient in the bad old days about to be cut open without anything to dull the pain.

"I couldn't have been less accurate. The cystoscopy was not in the least bit painful or horrific. My legs were supported in the air by props, but all intimate areas except the one necessary for the investigation were carefully covered over with green cloths. The nearest I came to discomfort was a slight feeling of 'urinating backwards' (as the surgeon put it) when I presume some anesthetizing gel was inserted into the urethra. The surgeon, nurses, and I talked among ourselves, and the surgeon told me exactly what he was going to do before he did it. The three or four minutes were neither unpleasant nor frightening. I could have kicked myself for taking accounts from people who had not actually experienced this investigation themselves, counting them as gospel truth. When I reemerged from the operating room, I told the nurse how painless the experience had been and asked her why she had thought it would be painful. She replied, 'I just thought that it would be painful if people started sticking instruments into my bladder!' For someone who dislikes anesthetics I would say if you don't mind your legs in the air for a few minutes, have your cystoscopy with a local anesthetic, and there is nothing at all to fear."

A cystoscopy is a minor operation usually done under general anesthetic with an instrument called a cystoscope. This enables the urologist to look into your bladder and examine the quality of the skin and the urine. Insertion of the instrument also tells the urologist whether he is looking at a frequently infected woman or a healthy woman. It will open up old urethral scars as it is inserted, and the smears of blood which come away together with thickened skin are indicative of frequent infections.

Make no mistake, it hurts to pass urine for the first time after a cystoscopy. Use the self-help management process, and treat it as a forthcoming cystitis attack; it's the only way to relieve the pain. When the urologist finds evidence of frequent infections, he has a choice of treatments. He can either immediately cauterize (burn away) the infected skin or prescribe prolonged antibiotic treatment. Neither is really helpful.

So it's back to the family doctor who won't be pleased to see you return without improvement after all his referrals. He cannot think what else to do. The textbook impells him to believe that because all the tests are negative or unresponsive to antibiotics, you are really making a fuss about a very small complaint. Perhaps you are even beginning to imagine it.

"But, Doctor, I can't be imagining blood, can I?"

He's foxed, but he shouldn't be.

Since more women than men suffer from cystitis, could the reproductive organs perhaps offer an answer? At this point it must be stressed that investigation into the causes of cystitis in a gynecology department is still very much avant-garde. The idea is only just beginning to take root in specialists' minds, but a few enlightened urology units do employ a gynecologist within the department for such investigations.

If your family doctor fails to refer you to a gynecologist, insist on it. A smiling face requesting this referral goes down better with the harassed family

doctor than a noisy demand but if that becomes necessary, try it. If not, sit in, or find a new doctor with
his own microscope. Even try your nearest VD unit,
where you need no referral letter for a vaginal
checkup. It is not quite as thorough in looking for
unusual causes as a hospital's gynecology unit, but it
will pick up all troublesome discharges and cervical
problems and may refer you to the other unit if the
venereologist is unhappy about something.

*The majority of background causes for recur-
rent attacks of cystitis lie in the reproductive organs.*
(Read that again.) If self-help prevention fails,
go back for more gynecological examinations. See
several gynecologists if necessary, and have a
healthy respect for your reproductive system's abili-
ty to hide its troubles. What looks healthy to one
specialist's eyes is a downright glaring condition to
another.

This is all very difficult if you happen to live in
an isolated area or a large area served by one small
hospital without proper equipment and up-to-the-
minute ideas. You may have to travel far away and
perhaps pay a great deal of money for an honest
medical detective. If you are suffering enough, you
will. If you cannot afford such help, what then? By
having even the simplest tests and examinations the
patient can feel reassured that nothing substantially
bad is wrong with her. She and her doctor must get
together for talks and fact-finding sessions. She
needs to make notes about her attacks and to think
of anything at all which could have triggered them
off. Trying to prevent them is all-important, as we
shall later discover, but if you really are what is
called a hard-core case without good health insur-

ance or private monetary means, then you are in the lap of the gods. Fortunately you really are a tiny minority, and the majority can take heart that gynecologist, urologist, and this book will sort your problem(s) out.

4. Cystitis in Childhood

Those people who believe that cystitis is an adult illness, and a sexual adult illness at that, have something more to learn. If there is one thing worse than sitting on the toilet in great pain by yourself, it is watching the screaming child doing it on a potty. Mother feels useless and frustrated, angry, and emotional. She may be trying to grapple with a problem about which she has no ideas, no knowledge, and no experience. There is no advice for her except the very one-sided medical viewpoint and not much pediatric advice other than that accompanying any surgery.

The same rule of symptom/cause can be applied. Your child, whatever her age, has a cause for her attacks just as a grown woman does. Cystitis is there because something somewhere is wrong. Childhood cystitis is a great deal easier to sort out because one can eliminate such backgrounds as the multitude of sexual causes, operations gone wrong, and others of gynecological origin.

As with adults, attacks recur, and your child must be given all hospital tests as soon as the pattern of recurrency is established. Very roughly, the cause of cystitis in children can be found in the following areas:

- The kidneys, ureters, bladder, urethra
- External contamination by toiletries
- Haphazard hygiene routines
- Poor liquid intake

The commonest children's kidney trouble is a condition called a refluxing ureter. Briefly it means that one or both of the two sphincter valves which allow urine through to the bladder from the ureters are not working correctly. Refluxing ureters shut off before all the collecting urine has had time to pass through to the bladder. When they shut off, some urine remains trapped in the ureter, and over a period of time this urine becomes stale and may provide a breeding ground for infection to start.

After this diagnosis has been made by IVP, medical care tries to mark time for as long as possible. By the time the child is nine it is generally held that a refluxing ureter sometimes "grows out of it." The ureter grows in pace with the child's general growth and sorts itself out. This doesn't always work, but usually the pediatrician (children's specialist) and his department keep a close watch on progress and are ready to operate quickly if it becomes obvious that the child is failing to thrive. They will be looking for inadequate weight gain, inadequate growth, lethargy, and continual infection.

These days, with plastic and nylon being such adaptable products, children who have to be operated on for refluxing ureter are given specially suitable plastic replacements. The replacement ureter is said to last forever and to expand in conjunction with the child's growth so that further operations are unnecessary.

Obviously, attention in a good children's hospital not only gives the very best medical care under these circumstances but also gives the mother more confidence. She doesn't have the tiny nagging thought that perhaps the doctor doesn't understand her child too well. In a children's hospital the staff deals solely with children and does understand.

Naturally the IVP will pick up any other kidney trouble as well. There are people born with one kidney and others with four—it's uncommon certainly, but it has been documented.

If your child has been given an IVP and good attentive pediatric care with negative results showing frequently, then you must turn your attention away from medical causes for your child's attacks and work on another theory.

"Am I possibly causing my child's cystitis? How can I find out?"

There is no possible way at present that you can find out easily except in this book. Many mothers have found occasional little tips on dealing with their children's cystitis but usually never explore the self-help as fully as they might.

Admitting that you could be causing it is a brave step, but it leaves the way open for questioning every single action you take in each daily routine.

Here is a checklist. Think about each one very carefully; a quick skim through might make you miss something you could investigate more fully.

- Are you using a biological washing powder? These are far too strong on a baby's skin.
- Are you using a launderette and its powder for laundering diapers?
  Again the cause may be chemical contamination.
- Are you giving your baby too much fruit juice? If the baby eats fruit puddings, fruit juices may be unnecessary.
- What creams are you using on the baby's tender vaginal area?

Mothers are easily persuaded by manufacturers eager for profits. A normal baby needs only a thin smear of zinc and castor-oil cream around its back passage. If you use a modern diaper liner, which allows urine through but keeps the baby's skin dry, you don't need to do anything further unless a severe rash develops. If this happens, cut out all fruit and give the baby boiled cool water; also expose the bottom to air at all times except at night.

- With which soap are you washing her bottom? The tiniest amount of nonmedicated soap should be used and washed off immediately. Truthfully, just the warm bath water is sufficient anyway.
- Are you adding antiseptic to the baby's bath? Don't! It's far too strong and quite unnecessary.
- Once she is out of diapers, what sort of pants does your child wear?

"I mentioned in my previous letter that my granddaughter aged five years had just had a bad attack of cystitis. The clinic doctor advised cotton pants, and it might interest you to know that afterward on two occasions in the morning rush for school she put on navy blue panties and again complained later of a pain in her bottom. It was only on the second occasion that my daughter realized what had happened. On mentioning this to our lady doctor, she was told that not only may the nylon cause irritation, but the sealing agent in the navy blue dye may irritate the urethra and precipitate an attack. She now wears only white cotton and has had no more trouble."

Nylon pants are very, very bad for small girls.

- Do you wash your child's hair in the bath?
  Shampoos are chemicals. They can contaminate and irritate tender areas like eyes, and they do the same on little bottoms. If your child is too small to have her hair washed over the basin, then wash it in a shallow bath, and rinse it off with jugfuls of fresh water. Rinse her bottom off as well. Empty the bath, rinse it out, and then run her normal bath. Improvise in any way, but keep the shampoo away from her bottom.
- What soap does your little girl use?
  Don't use anything highly perfumed or medicated. Keep the bath from becoming too soapy, and remember that plain water is always safe.
- Do well-meaning people pour bubble bath into your child's bath?
  Again it's a chemical and easily contaminates a tender bottom. So does dishwashing liquid used as a bubble bath.
- Does cystitis occur in your child a few hours after swimming?
  It is chlorine irritation. A shower afterward reduces the risk.

- Do attacks occur in the summer?
  Soft acidic fruits such as strawberries and raspberries can cause soreness and burning urine. Limit the fruit, and increase liquids.
- Is your laundry soap too strong?
  Use a mild brand, and rinse the underwear several times.
- Could she have a hereditary skin sensitivity?
  It doesn't have to mean a spotty skin or eczema. Check in your family.
- Have you taught her to wipe her bottom from front to back so that germs are kept away from the urethra?
  It's never too early to teach this basic hygiene technique.
- What are the drinking arrangements at school?
  Pressure on teachers and helpers often means that water and milk are neglected.

> "My daughter went from a cup of tea at eight in the morning to four in the afternoon with no drink. The teachers were too busy, and my daughter hates the water fountain in the playground."

Ask your child daily what she has drunk at school. If she has not had the equivalent of three glasses of drink at the very least during school hours, go to the principal. Strong-colored, smelly, burning urine is always improved by a good water intake and the burning will stop.

Once in her teens, she may start attacks of cystitis or even worsen the attacks she has had as a child if her existing cause isn't yet located.

- Are her cotton pants being changed daily?
  Vaginal secretions start in puberty and, if allowed to become stale, will cause soreness and even harbor infections.
- Are her periods failing to settle down?
  Two years at the outside of irregularity and excessive pain need investigation. Choose a youngish but experienced female gynecologist or anyone well known for work with hormones in premenstrual trouble. Read *The Menstrual Cycle* by Dr. Katherina Dalton, or any good book on menstrual problems.
- Does she cry before a period, swell up, and become overemotional?
  She may need mild hormone help. Don't be fobbed off if your instinct tells you that the girl needs some kind of gynecological help.
- Are all the toiletry, washing, and chemical rules still being observed?
  Teenage girls love to experiment with toiletries and deodorants, but if it is at the expense of their health, they must be made to realize it. Give her this to read.
- What menstrual protection is she using?
  Tampons can cause trouble. They're drying, contain mild chemicals in the cotton, are difficult for teenagers to insert without nicking the vaginal skin, and the string can promote infection. Pads are less of a problem, unless they are chemically deodorized or with plastic backing.
- Has she secretly started taking the Pill?
  Once on this and having sex, she belongs in the adult sexual sections of this book no matter what her age.

These checklists should stimulate your thoughts. Maybe you are doing something else to your child which is not on these lists. Think, and by way of experiment remove the routine in doubt and note any changes in your child. While you are sorting out doubtful routines and concentrating on eliminating possible causes, it's quite possible that attacks of cystitis, soreness, or burning urine are still occurring. You cannot pour a half pint of liquid down a five-year-old's throat every twenty minutes, so here is a modified version of the self-help management process. Emphasis is on getting the child to drink happily and to be prepared to pass urine for rewards or bribes.

- Find an unusual drinking receptacle like a souvenir eggcup or a pretty pink glass or a mug with a poem written around it—anything that interests the child to handle and drink from. Change it when boredom sets in during the three hours.
- Get as much liquid as you can into the child without wearing her temper. Let her rest for fifteen minutes or so, and then have another liquid session. Keep it up for as long as possible, aiming at three hours.
- Vary the flavors of drink, but remember that all should be 98 percent water and only flavored or colored to pretend it is exciting. Serve the drinks up hot, warm, or very cold to tempt the child. Intersperse a glass of milk or a very weak, sugary tea.
- Use one-quarter teaspoon of bicarbonate of soda—no more—in one of these drinks or in a teaspoon of favorite jam. Give an initial dose

and then one more only an hour and a half later.

- If bicarbonate is unacceptable, try potassium citrate in a dose approved by your doctor or consultant.

- With all that liquid going down the child's stomach a Tylenol tablet will do no harm. Use just one at the start of the attack crushed in jam and then another after two or three hours if the child is still distressed.

- Put your child to bed or to rest near you on the sofa with the potty handy.

- Give her a warm hot-water bottle to cuddle. Keep her own special one, perhaps in an animal shape that is a novelty.

- If praise is sufficient for your child when she sits on the potty and passes urine, then praise her highly. If she's intelligent enough to understand what you are trying to do with all this intake of water and subsequent passing of urine, explain simply and with a smile of confidence. She will respond and learn from you not to be afraid of the attack. If you have a child used to being bribed, try to ration the bribe, a sweet or favorite story, so that interest lasts to the three hours if possible.

- Gently wipe the child's bottom front to back with warm, moist cotton, and look for signs of redness. If there is inflammation, it could be anything. Try zinc and castor-oil cream around the back passage or on the legs, but on no account put any near her urethral or vaginal openings.

- Go to the doctor if the attack doesn't abate or worsens; but you are doing very well if the flushing-through process is working, and your doctor will be very pleased.

You might also gain some confidence and feel less alone in helping your child if you know that other mothers struggle in the same way. Here are some letters from mothers and a child indicating their troubles but written before they had any self-help advice:

"My daughter is four years old. Last year she had a kidney infection which cleared up after treatment from the doctor. However, since then she has suffered on a number of occasions from backaches, followed by frequent visits to the bathroom which lead to a burning sensation and a lot of discomfort for her. I have, of course, been back to the doctor, but he assures me there is no kidney infection and will not be pinned down as to a direct cause. His advice is to give her plenty of drink. A friend of mine who has suffered cystitis all her married life tells me the symptoms sound exactly the same, but as I have never heard of a child suffering this, I am not sure. Doctors are such touchy people, so I am wary of telling him my thoughts and am wondering if you could confirm whether little girls can suffer from cystitis, and any practical help you can give me would be much appreciated."

From Karen, aged eleven years:

"I am eleven years old and have had cystitis since I was six. Because of the attacks I have had two operations, one to have two tubes [probably ureters] moved into new positions and the second to have one of my kidneys removed. This was over a year ago; but I am still getting attacks of cystitis, and I hoped you could give me some new suggestions."

"I should be interested in any information or help you give to sufferers. I feel doubly qualified since I myself first had cystitis some ten months ago and have had about a dozen similar attacks since. Also, more important to me at the moment is my daughter's case. At two and a half years she has this September been *very* ill and was admitted to hospital with an undiagnosed complaint, which turned out to be a urinary infection. She has had various tests and investigations and, although well in herself, is still under the care of the outpatients' department at the hospital and will have to be on antibiotics for long term. I was told she must be kept on the medicine indefinitely, or else the infection will recur and could spread to the kidneys. It is most worrying for me that she should, at this age, have to be on medicine and also that they have told me she should just grow out of it, which seems rather vague."

"I came to know of your work through the mother of a little girl who was in hospital with my daughter. Both our children are having the same treatment with the same consultant, and it has been helpful to discuss our problems together."

"I have a young daughter aged nine years who has had cystitis for some time now. I feel so often completely alone in the process of coping with such distress in a child that I would like to get to know a couple of mothers near my home who are also struggling with cystitis in a child."

Attacks of cystitis are rare in boys. Usually a kidney abnormality is behind the symptoms. Little girls are open to infections and inflammations, being made as they are, and their skin around the urethra and vaginal openings is extremely tender. It canno be stressed too strongly how important mother and her routines are. Nursery schools and play groups should be regarded as potential hazards if your child suffers from cystitis. Helpers there cannot oversee the toilet arrangements with the same care that a mother does.

"As regards young children I have found by experience that when five-year-olds start school, they are often so frightened that they do not go to the toilet at school all day long. They often do not drink their milk and do not like the water which is served with their school dinner as they find it 'dirty.' After school their concentrated urine sets up an irritation. I know teachers are there primarily to do just that, but perhaps this is where mothers could help at school on a voluntary basis in the general care of the very young. It is sad to think that any child should suffer the misery of cystitis."

5. Liquid Intake, Acidity, and Diet

Not all so-called cystitis is true cystitis. Remember the three main symptoms of pain, frequency, and bleeding. Unfortunately just the spoken phrase "My urine is burning" is enough to send a doctor flying for his prescription pad while telling the patient that she has cystitis.

Burning urine by itself is not totally indicative of infection or inflammation, so great disappointment ensues when your carefully taken urine specimen turns out to be negative. The majority of doctors will still authorize antibiotics. The doctor knows you are *expecting* a prescription and might react hostilely if you don't get one, so he staves off an argument.

To know more about burning or scalding urine and how it gets like that, we have to understand what normal urine is. Normal urine is certainly a yardstick. It doesn't hurt, doesn't tingle, doesn't burn, and doesn't scald. When *your* urine is like that, your urine is normal for you. If at such a period of well-being you care to examine it, you will find it a topaz color, golden brown probably or even paler, sometimes colorless. It will mix well in the toilet bowl with the water and remain clear. Closer examination in a small glass jar will show how clear it really is. It doesn't smell at all, or just very faintly.

Urine that burns drops to the bottom of the toilet bowl. It smells horrible, hurts to pass, and the amount which you pass is usually small. It is often—in fact, always—brown, and if you feel like keeping a shallow saucer of it for a day or so, you will notice that after evaporation a thin film of crystal has formed. This crystal is uric acid.

Uric acid is manufactured in the kidneys and passes down with the liquid and waste products all together in urine to the bladder.

Burning urine doesn't necessarily hold excessive uric acid; rather, it hasn't got a large enough water content to dilute it. Some women do manufacture too much acid in their kidneys, but they are the rare exception rather than the rule.

Normal urine will always contain uric acid because that is its composition. If you tried to eradicate it, the best you could hope to achieve would be temporary alkalinity or very diluted urine for a few hours, no more. The kidneys will go on manufacturing uric acid whether you like it or not, and you must learn to control its effect if you become uncomfortable when passing urine.

If you find that most of your days are spent with the constant urge to go to the bathroom, it may be because the uric-acid content in your urine is abnormal and is upsetting the bladder nerves. Nerve endings are very close to the surface in the bladder. They have to be, in order to give you plenty of warning that emptying is necessary or else it will burst!) Because of this, the bladder will react to acid which simply heats up the nerve endings into an excitement. This excitement gives you the urge to urinate, yet when you get to the toilet, you pass only a small amount. Unless you start drinking lots of water in order to dilute the concentrated uric acid, the remaining crystals in your bladder will excite it still more, and you will have to go to the toilet again shortly.

It is interesting that the doctors who, in testing a patient's urine and regularly finding it to be over-acid, decide to stop antibiotics, then turn to tranquilizers with the intention of calming the nerve endings into near immobility.

For women who have great trouble when traveling, a bladder tranquilizer before the journey can be helpful, but this shouldn't have to apply on a daily basis. As some people's stomachs turn queasy during travel, so some women's bladders turn "tetchy" or "irritable."

"All holidays taken during the last five years have been a misery with symptoms similar to cystitis. My doctor gave me masses of antibiotics to swallow until we caught on to the idea that travel vibration seemed to trigger it off."

- Drink a couple of glasses of water before the journey.
- Take a level teaspoon of bicarbonate of soda to reduce and equate the uric acid.
- Take a Valium tablet to calm the bladder nerve endings.
- Sit on a large cushion to minimize vibration.

A daily or regular intake of Valium is habit-forming and unnecessary. Why is tap water, an excellent bladder calmer, so unfashionable these days? There's nothing wrong with it. It is as clean as can be in large Western cities, and if you have heard to the contrary, then boil it or use one of the large variety of bottled waters.

If more than one member of the family has regular kidney or bladder infections, it does no harm to phone the health and hygiene department of your local government offices and request a whole-house tap-water survey.

An average day's liquid intake should contain three to four pints of water either neat or in very weak tea, coffee, milk, or fruit sodas. Years ago, people drank simpler liquids than we do these days. They didn't bombard their kidneys with concentrated juices, coffees, teas, or large quantities of alcoholic beverages. Tap water is also the cheapest way of drinking and the cheapest, most effective way of ensuring healthy kidneys and bladder.

Young people drink colas and coffee all day, it seems. Water is certainly a large ingredient of these drinks, but many chemicals are added as well. It will be interesting in about twenty years' time to see whether the urology units have an increased waiting list and whether the dialysis units have been extended.

If you are not sure whether your urine is too acid, you can test it. Easily done by anyone, the test involves buying red or blue litmus papers from a drugstore. Tear one paper off the pack, and dip it in your urine sample.

A red litmus paper will remain red or thereabouts if your urine is overacidic. By turning to pinkish blue shades, it denotes a near normal acid content, and by turning blue, it denotes alkalinity (the opposite of acidity).

A blue litmus paper will turn pinkish blue, showing the urine to be normally mildly acidic, but if it goes beyond pinkish blue into a red, then the urine is overacidic.

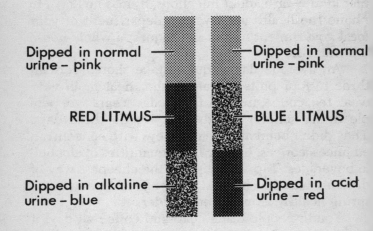

Dipped in normal urine – pink

Dipped in normal urine – pink

RED LITMUS

BLUE LITMUS

Dipped in alkaline urine – blue

Dipped in acid urine – red

Regular reddish hues after your second visit to the toilet each morning means you aren't drinking enough. Regular reddish hues of the litmus paper on your *first* urine sample of the morning *coupled with* burning or scalding mean there is insufficient liquid in the bladder, but it may also mean that a level tea spoonful of bicarbonate of soda at night (heart pa tients excepted) could be helpful. It doesn't have to be taken every night, particularly if you help the bladder well enough in daytime. But some women particularly older ones, find this tip helpful and i also decreases the need to pass urine during the night.

Again, if bicarbonate makes you feel queasy, use potassium citrate instead.

One of the oldest known reasons for attacks of cystitis given by women to their doctors or by doctors to their patients is "I/you have a chill in my/your waterworks." "A chill in the bladder," "a chill in the kidneys." Some women will tie it in with standing at a cold, windy bus stop, gardening in the late evening, or simply sitting on a cold stone.

> "The attacks became more and more frequent, but I began to make observations that each time I had cystitis I could always recall being chilled either at the bottom of my back or directly on the opening of the urethra. I told my doctor this, but he firmly replied that cystitis is a germ which multiplies. Some months later I had another attack but, being on vacation, had to see a lady doctor, who agreed with my thoughts of catching a chill. So from then on I was able to trace many more attacks to a chill and learned to keep my back and bottom warm."

This patient has discovered what triggers her attacks but has failed to follow the thought process through scientifically.

Because such women have no idea of what immediate action to take, they do nothing about it except visit the toilet more and more frequently over the next few hours. In twenty-four to thirty-six hours' time they are possibly feverish and shivery and have a backache, so off they go to visit their doctors.

If an MSU is taken, it will reveal nothing bacterial but may come back specifying excess acidity. By then the doctor will have begun the broad-spectrum antibiotic and played safe in case it was an infection. As the patient has already started the course, she will be requested to "finish it anyway."

Understanding the real reason why such women need to go to the doctor after "waiting at a windy bus stop" negates the need for drugs.

What the patient has done is to excite her bladder nerve endings and urethral nerve endings. More accurately, she hasn't—the cold wind has. Anyone who waits at a cold, windy bus stop has a strong urge to pass urine the minute she arrives home. So she goes to the toilet and passes a lot of urine, but after half an hour she wants to go again, and she does. There is not so much urine this time. The patient with a tetchy bladder now has little liquid in her body, so the kidneys, still busy manufacturing uric acid, can find no water with which to dilute it. Down in the bladder uric-acid concentrate adds to the excitement caused initially by the cold wind and a generally chilly, shivery body. With dual excitement, the bladder and urethral nerve endings come to such a state that the patient constantly feels the need to pass urine.

At that point she is convinced that she has an attack of cystitis from catching a chill. She only has two out of the three symptoms, though, not yet the bleeding, but that can come once the uric acid is concentrated enough to burn open the previous urethral scars.

Clearly there is no infection, but how can she extricate herself from such a mess?

Apart from her instantly getting into a hot bath to warm up herself as well as her urethra, it is not possible to calm down the excited bladder nerv endings quickly. More important, and more sensibly, she must drink liquid to give the kidneys water with which to dilute the uric acid. A hot drink is an excellent idea, but nothing strong—only very weak chocolate, tea, or coffee. (Alcohol at this time can only triple the excitement, so don't even *consider* a hot toddy!) Tap water will do a quicker and equally thorough job since by the time the kidneys make contact with the liquid it is hardly hot anymore.

Several drinks are necessary before the cold, excited bladder starts to calm down, and at the earliest possible moment, i.e., arrival inside the front door— a glass of water, followed shortly afterward by a long hot drink, could be sufficient. If not, then perhaps two pints may have to be consumed.

The action of coffee, tea, and alcohol is one of exciting the kidneys into producing urine in response to the amount drunk. Both coffee and tea contain caffeine. Tea leaves contain about 2 to 4 percent, while coffee beans have about half that amount, but since coffee is usually drunk in a much stronger form, it proves the more hazardous.

Drinking strong coffee throughout the day stimulates the urge to urinate. Each emptying of the bladder leaves minute quantities of caffeine behind to irritate still further, and generous water washouts are the only way to flush the particles through. The kidneys have deposits of caffeine to reject as well, and several mugs of strong coffee each day prove quite wearing. Coffee taken in the late evening as a bedtime drink could keep you awake some hours until its effect on the kidneys and bladder died away. Such a simple action can be a cause of nocturnal trips to the toilet and a tired person the next morning. Something as simple as that can also be behind visits to the hospital to "sort out my frequency."

Tea, if drunk strong and in quantity, will do just the same. One woman reports:

> "Regarding tea and coffee, I have found it very difficult to know what to drink in their place but, on consulting a naturopath, was again told no tea, no coffee—because it caused acidity in the blood. I was told that dandelion coffee does not contain this acid, and the only acid-free tea is Brazilian herb tea, best drunk with a slice of lemon or spoonful of honey."

Women with weak, tetchy bladders should never drink strong coffee or tea. Young women subject to attacks of true cystitis or frequency should not drink them either. All efforts to refrain from temptation can be met by psychological coloring of the mug with only a coffeespoonful of a weak blend. The first cup out of the pot of tea is always the weakest, so be first in line.

Modern life would feel miserable if complete denial or abstinence from tea and coffee drinking were demanded, but do be very sensible in the amount of these two beverages and their strength.

Alcohol is largely an irritant. It is absorbed into the blood vessels and body tissues while journeying through the stomach and the upper part of the small intestine. It converts into heat and becomes an irritant to the kidneys and bladder, which abound with blood vessels and nerve endings. A single glass of wine or six pints of beer can produce a frequency effect. As long as you learn your limits and are prepared to drink a couple of glasses of water, to deexcite the nerve endings, that's all right. Obviously whiskey and gin can start most cystitis patients or the bathroom road quite quickly. An occasional glass of weak alcoholic beverage is less likely to affect the bladder, though many patients are better in complete abstinence.

Find your own tolerance level, and take action to counteract trouble. If you are on a real binge like a party or wedding, try a level teaspoonful of bicarbonate and a glass of fruit soda before you depart to give the kidneys a cushion.

Drink and sex together are horrendous troublemakers, so watch out!

Food can be important to some cystitis patients, but for some reason many women become besotted with dietary worries. In cystitis this is not a large enough influence to make significant recurrent trouble. Citrus fruits, soft fruits like strawberries, hot curries several times a week, or lots of black pepper on every meal will naturally create some excitability in a tetchy bladder. A good strawberry season for devotees of this delicious fruit will heighten the uric-acid content substantially, and in the summers of 1975 and 1976 many British women had to have medical help for cystitis. They need not have since lots of water and a teaspoon of bicarbonate would have done the trick much better.

Some women's bladders prefer not to have to excrete starch or glucose, and these two products are usually derivatives of white flour, white sugar, cakes, bread, biscuits, cookies, jams, sweet drinks, chocolate, and sweets. If you think you have been everywhere and done everything to relieve your bladder troubles, try refusing these items or any food containing refined starch and sugars. Some women have improved on this regimen and so have many men.

I want to make it clear that the use of dietary measures to control bladder weakness is of value only in those cases where infection is *not* present, i.e., where there is frequency, urgency, or stress incontinence but no pain. A British doctor reports:

> "I had in my practice at that time a girl in her middle thirties suffering from frequency and urgency of micturition with stress incontinence, for which no cause or cure could be found. She had been investigated at the National Hospital for Nervous Diseases, where they could find no neurological cause for her symptoms. She had been investigated in Kingston Hospital by the gynecologist and by the genitourinary surgeon, who could equally find no abnormality. She had had physiotherapy to her perineal muscles without effect. I put her on a 'gluten-free' diet and she had, within ten days, relief from her symptoms. Since then I have kept an eye open for other cases of loss of or poor bladder control in the *absence of infection* and have successfully treated some fifty cases with a diet free from cereals, onions, and beans.
>
> "It is not generally accepted that there is some protein factor—the precise nature of which is not yet known—present in wheat which causes, in a susceptible person, the malabsorption of food, minerals, and vitamins of the B group. It is known that this illness is usually associated with damage to the nervous system, including irritability and depression among its central effects and neuritis among its peripheral effects. It is this peripheral effect which causes poor nerve control of the bladder and in some cases of the rectal sphincter also. I have found eight of these latter in the past ten years."

There is currently no certain laboratory test to determine whether or not diet is a factor. The *only* satisfactory test lies in excluding the suspect foods and finding the symptoms disappear only to have them recur when a normal diet is resumed.

The test diet must exclude all wheat, rye, corn, oats, and barley and their derivatives, which include grain alcohols, liquid glucose, and vegetable fats— i.e., all the margarines and cooking oils (with the exception of olive oil). The onion family, the bean family—especially ground nuts (peanuts), and the cocoa bean (cocoa and chocolate)—must also be excluded.

It must be noted that virtually all commercial cakes, candy bars, and cookies contain flour, glucose syrup, or chocolate.

The diet is of necessity plain in the early stages, and starch is represented by potatoes, rice, tapioca, and sugar (not soft brown), which must be taken in amounts adequate to make up for the missing bread and cakes. Meat, fish, cheese, butter, eggs, fresh fruits or canned fruits free from glucose, green and root vegetables, excluding only the bean group and the onion group, are all freely permitted. A suggestion of dishes for the various meals of the day may be found on pp. 59–62. If this diet is *strictly* adhered to for a week or ten days, and it is going to be successful, it will have succeeded by then.

If normal bladder control is regained—the normal bladder does not get you up at night, and daytime frequency should be but two or three times for a female, four or five times for a male—without urgency, precipitancy, or stress incontinence, the dietary regimen should be continued for at least two weeks, so that one can be satisfied that the bladder control achieved is not just temporary. Then adequate amounts of cereals, onions, beans, and sweets should be taken for two days to establish that loss of control does recur and, thus, that the improvement has been definitely related to the diet and not to the "grace of God." This having been established, return to the strict diet to regain control.

It is then often possible to widen the diet by the inclusion of barley, corn, and oats, which may not contain enough of the toxic protein to matter to the individual person. It is important to realize that each individual person has his own personal degree of tolerance and that this will deteriorate under stress (illness, overwork, or worry).

Substitutes for ordinary bread and biscuits which *may* be safe to eat are the gluten-free breads and biscuits, but it must be stressed that they are not protein-*free*, and it is the protein in the cereals which carries the toxic factor; some people may therefore be unable to tolerate them.

There is one other substance which may be responsible—either alone or as an addition to the cereal factor—for bladder weakness. This is lactose, the sugar normally present in milk—"cow sugar."

Those who are intolerant to lactose will already be taking milk only in small amounts and only when disguised in tea, coffee, Ovaltine, or one of the other "milky" drinks.

People who have this intolerance can replace whole milk by single or double cream or by the "top of the milk." Butter and cheese (not blue cheese) are perfectly safe to eat.

There are two low-lactose milks available, and these may safely be used by those who have *only* lactose intolerance; they are *not* suitable for those people who have a cereal intolerance as well. Canned or powdered milks are *not* suitable.

Again, a trial period of ten days is adequate—if

the diet is strict—to assess response. There is a reliable laboratory test—the lactose tolerance curve—for this condition.*

SPECIMEN DIET

Breakfast

Fruit juice, grapefruit, or stewed fruit

* * *

Boiled egg
Egg and bacon
Kidneys, bacon, and tomato
Ham and eggs (poached, fried, or scrambled)
Omelet
Smoked haddock with butter
Kippers (fried or grilled)

* * *

Toasted gluten-free bread } with butter
or rolls
Gluten-free biscuits
Marmalade (if allowed)
Honey

* * *

Coffee or tea with cream or milk and sugar

* * *

*For further reading, see *Are You Allergic?* by William G. Crook, M.D., published by Professional Books, P. O. Box 3494, Jackson, Tennessee 38301.

Packed Lunch

Homemade soup in Thermos

Cheese ⎫ Ham ⎪ Corned beef ⎬ Pork ⎪ Hard-boiled eggs ⎭	With salad prepared in plastic container OR Gluten-free biscuits and butter
Hamburger patties	gluten-free pastry
Cheese and apple ⎫ Cooked soft roes ⎬ Sardines in olive oil ⎪ Salmon ⎭	Spread on gluten-free biscuits

* * *

Fresh fruit
Yogurt

* * *

Milk or coffee

Light Lunch

Boiled rice with kidneys and bacon	
Fish	Can all be served
Omelet	on gluten-free toast

Cheese and potato pie
Cheese balls and tomatoes
Various salads
Poached or scrambled eggs
Toasted cheese on ham

* * *

Fresh or canned fruit

Lunch or Dinner

Homemade soup
Fruit juice
Melon
Grapefruit

*   *   *

Roast chicken, lamb, beef, or pork
Baked ham and pineapple
Chops or steak (grilled or fried)
Liver and bacon
Fish
Casserole of beef, lamb, or chicken
Grilled ham steak
Escalope of veal (dipped in egg and ground almonds)

*   *   *

Potatoes (roasted, baked in jacket, boiled, or fried)
Boiled rice
Any other vegetables except green beans or onions
Salads

*   *   *

Rice, sago, or tapioca pudding
Egg custard
Caramel cream
Chestnut mousse
Coffee crème
Canned, dried, or stewed fruit
Coconut sponge with syrup
Almond sponge with apricot jam

Almond gâteau
Apple macaroon
Raspberry ratafia meringue
Steamed sponge pudding
Junket
Apple or other stewed fruit with meringue

* * *

Cheese and butter

The flour used for the above dishes *must* be "gluten-free" rice flour, potato flour, or soya flour.

It is not always possible to know whether what you are drinking is actually being passed out, and sometimes this becomes necessary in a fully comprehensive diagnosis. In such a case, where the specialist needs to know the amount of liquid intake and whether the kidneys and bladder are excreting an approximate amount, he authorizes a chart. The patient is requested to choose a drinking vessel like a half-pint mug in which it is easy to be accurate in a given amount for each drink. Whatever she drinks and whenever she drinks are marked on the chart, and she is requested for four days to act as usual. The specialist can then see if his patient is doing anything stupid in her drinking habits. He can also see if the bladder could be expected to behave well under those circumstances.

The currently fashionable trend of not drinking much water must be halted. Our bodies will not survive without water, and our urology units and general practice units would be a little less busy if the trend were reversed.

6. Washing

Escherichia coli, E. coli for short, is a very common germ often found in the urine samples of women who have cystitis. Medicine has based much of its research and drug treatments on this germ, and it is largely the reason why doctors reach for a prescription pad to treat a patient undergoing a cystitis attack. It is one of the many inhabitants of the bowel and normally lives quite placidly there.

When a stool is passed, or the patient is having an attack of diarrhea or, also common, anal hemorrhoids after childbirth, this germ contaminates other areas. Wiping with soft toilet paper carefully is insufficient, and as soon as the panties are pulled up and skin contact is made, the germ spreads.

Unless mothers teach their daughters to wipe their bottoms from front to back, little girls will get cystitis from *E. coli* just as much as adults.

A particularly hazardous time of the day for younger women to have intercourse is the late evening if they have failed to decontaminate the perineal area after a bowel movement earlier in the day. Bathing after intercourse in this instance cannot undo the damage. During intercourse *E. coli* is massaged into the urethra or vagina and is once more in a dark, moist, warm environment like its original home. It is not possible to eradicate *E. coli* from the bowel, so don't be misled by a doctor who says that antibiotics will eradicate the germs. One does not try to eradicate saliva from the mouth! More important and more possible are attempts to confine *E. coli* to its domain within the bowels.

If external hemorrhoids or diarrhea are present, these conditions should be treated, but the everyday use of a simple washing routine is applicable to everyone. It is not a question of how often you wash but *when* you wash.

In the days before toilet paper, newspaper was commonly used. In order to wipe away the newsprint from her bottom, great-grandmama would have taken to the outhouse an old but clean cotton rag. This was wet with hot water, and if she was quick, it would still be nice and warm to use after her bowel movement. (People didn't loiter in outhouses, especially in cold weather!)

At night large china or porcelain commodes were available in all bedrooms, and water in a jug took the place of toilet paper. Great-grandmama kept and boiled her own pieces of rag in the boiler which all respectable sculleries housed at one time. Rags played a still larger part in her life.

There were no sanitary napkins or tampons, of course. Each woman, eighty years ago, made her own from soft old linen or cotton. She probably had five or six, which, after use, she would soak in cold water and then sterilize by boiling them for about twenty minutes. They would be dried discreetly in the oven or hung out on the clothesline.

Her pieces of rag may not appeal to us today, but that was all that was available in those times. Automatically great-grandmama was washing her bottom after a stool. Although toilet paper is a great advance, it has brought a certain amount of complacency in advanced hygiene. (There is, incidentally, much debate about the dyes used to color toilet tissue. The safest is undoubtedly white, but I have heard of medical evidence only against blue toilet tissue—no other colors seem to have attracted any medical comment.)

It is necessary for every woman, and cystitis sufferers in particular, to wash the perineum after passing a stool. Washing cannot sterilize your bottom, but it can remove renegade *E. coli* and avoid the possibility of urethral contamination.

E. coli thrives in normal, mildly acidic bladder urine because there is plenty of food in the waste products waiting to be passed out. The urine is warm and permits ease of travel around the bladder walls just as female lubricants permit sperm to arrive at their goal.

A morning bath or a late-night bath leaves the whole day for this rampant germ to explore your perineum. Therefore, you should be made aware of the measures to contain it when possible.

Washing your bottom is often a matter of improvisation. For instance, the way you do it in a squalid ladies' room is different from what you can do in the warmth and relaxation of your own bathroom, but even so the aim is to get water on your bottom several times.

Here are three suggestions. One can be classified as emergency, one for office and home, and the last perhaps for home only.

1. This can be easily achieved in the most public of conveniences and involves the use of either wads of toilet tissue or paper hankies from your bag. Please don't ever use antiseptic cleansing tissues— the chemical will irritate. After wiping yourself carefully with dry toilet paper, pull your pants up above your knees, but don't let them touch your bottom. Walk out to the nearest basin, and wash your hands well; then wet two wads of hankie or toilet tissue. Go back inside the toilet. With one lot wipe your perineum slowly and carefully front to back, and throw it down the toilet. Repeat with the other wad slowly and carefully; then flush the toilet, and arrange your clothing. For now, this is better than nothing and far preferable to smearing *E. coli* over your pants for the rest of the day.

2. If you work in an office, it is possible to keep a pretty toiletry bag somewhere, and even if you have no office but travel around in your job, it still doesn't entitle you to use manufactured cleansing tissues. Either use the previous method of washing or carry a facecloth in a plastic bag.

After you wipe the perineum as usual with toilet tissues, again wash your hands well in hot water, with soap. Wet a facecloth retained only for this purpose, and if you are out of the house, use this instead of the paper hankies.

The facecloth must be boiled before you use it the next day, and it should be boiled only in plain water, no washing powders at all.

If you decide to use this method at home, you can use a little plain soap only on your anus, not on the front parts, before you start to use the cloth.

Rinse it out between each wipe, and don't forget to boil it.

Cotton swabs could be used instead, but they are expensive and could stop up your household plumbing.

3. The third method is ideal for home and for women living in the tropics where tap water is so often contaminated.

Women in the tropics usually drink previously boiled and bottled water; sometimes it is filtered as well. Take a couple of bottles from the refrigerator, and keep them in the bathroom. After wiping the perineum front to back, part your legs and let the bottled water run backward from the labia to the anus. You can also stand up and gently soap only the anal area, then sit back again and let the sterile bottled water run over it. If you don't live in the tropics, you can still run warm tap water between your legs from an old glass bottle as you sit on the toilet, but it doesn't have to be boiled first.

Lots of women sit on a basin of water after passing a stool, but this is dangerous since *E. coli* mixes up in that small amount of water and can easily be washed into the urethra or vagina.

As for the bidet, which all Frenchwomen swear by, it is not available in every home, but in those where it does exist there is still the possibility of washing *E. coli* into the urethra even if a douche spray can be operated. *E. coli* on the cervix can usually be traced to a suspicious hygiene routine such as the previous two examples.

By far the safest way of all is to pour water between the labia and backward to the anus from either a jug or a bottle. In cases of diarrhea the process should be employed after every bowel movement.

Since the separation of facecloths from "bottom" cloths is essential in the actual washing process, so then is the separation of a body towel from a "bottom" towel. Frenchwomen's habits are important here. They keep linen napkins near their bidets simply for drying afterward. Patting dry is preferable to rubbing briskly, and the softer the towel, the better.

As well as washing after passing a stool, there are other times in the day when this process can be necessary. It is important that both the vaginal opening and the urethral opening are cleansed. Perhaps the boiled facecloth or a moist cotton swab may be more convenient, but usually the woman is partly or wholly undressed anyway, so the bottled water approach can still apply.

Safety-first occasions, which can sometimes be omitted if others are being rigidly enforced, take place first thing in the morning and last thing at night. Both sessions will freshen up the perineum, lessening the likelihood of stale odors. In very hot weather, cool or cold water on the perineum keeps it cool and odorless, and acts as a vaginitis preventive. Some kinds of discharges are best removed only by moist balls of cotton, since warm water only adds to the irritation and discomfort. Cotton balls clear it away, are disposable, and don't exacerbate the trouble.

Swimming is a danger to all women who suffer from cystitis. There are all sorts of things in the water. In a freshwater pool chlorine is the major hazard. Not only can it irritate, but regular daily dips for several weeks may unbalance the natural defenses of your vagina. A shower afterward is essential—make sure the clean water penetrates the

vagina as high as possible. With so much tap water
being chlorinated these days, a regular delivery of
spring water to your home, both for washing the
perineum and for drinking, ought to be money well
spent.

Sexually active women are foolish not to wash
before intercourse, whatever time of day or night it
takes place. This simple process performed before
sex can save three weeks in bed with pyelitis. Cool
or cold water is good to tone up the tissues before
play begins. The Japanese use the washing process
as part of their sexual rituals, and double bathing in
a warm room can be highly erotic, in turn stimulating as well as relaxing. (After-intercourse washing
will be dealt with a little later on.)

Douching of the vagina is now too controversial
for a hard-and-fast rule. Certainly more germs can
enter in douching than come out, but very occasionally a gynecologist may prescribe a gentian violet
douche, a weak vinegar douche, or a weak bicarbonate of soda douche. Never, never try douching yourself with antiseptic solution; you will hit the roof a
day later. *When you are using one of the three recommended washing routines, douching is absolutely unnecessary.*

Bathing may be wonderfully relaxing and
warming, with a great temptation to lie and soak,
but doing that more than once or twice a week can
be provocative to the urethra. Remember that ex-
tremes of heat and cold excite the nerve endings. In
a hot bath your perineum, kidneys, and pubic area
are all immersed in heat. Watch how your legs and
arms in a hot bath turn red and swell slightly as the
blood supply heats up. Have a five-minute soak if
you must once a week; but use the bath for washing

only on other occasions, and get out fairly quickly. (Hot water for a bath costs more than a bottle of water to wash your bottom even though it does the same job.)

Don't put anything at all in the bath except your body! Plain water without anything added is a safety-first feature, but also important is what might be in that bath before the water is run. Make sure you rinse the tub with plenty of water after you've scrubbed it—having residual cleansers or germicides lapping your vagina ought to be avoided.

Showering is safer in almost all respects than bathing, so if you can, get a shower unit installed.

Following a television lecture on cystitis, I received a good many letters from women who had discovered the importance of hygiene the hard way. Two examples follow:

> "Cystitis was making my life a misery with severe attacks about every two months. At every medical consultation I succeeded in annoying my doctor for what I considered to be proper tests. At every attack he was given a urine specimen, which he always ended up throwing down the sink until one day I insisted on a proper laboratory culture. He lost his temper, and I lost mine hearing him say that he hadn't the time to mess about sending specimens to path labs because they wouldn't give an accurate enough result. We exchanged a lot of rude words, and I left the room in tears. Since I worked in a blood transfusion laboratory and held a B.Sc. in biology, I decided to take my next specimen into the bacteriology lab and see for myself. I grew a beautiful *E. coli*, 'acquired' some antibiotics, and ended that attack. But since learning about hygiene tips, I have started prevention and am delighted to report

that I am now completely free of this lousy complaint. I changed my doctor and feel that women should stand up more for the correct and available tests."

"One point which I think was not brought up in your television program is that male doctors are probably somewhat embarrassed at explaining intimate details of feminine hygiene. Also I think that quite a number of patients would be rather offended if one asked too many questions about their personal cleanliness."

In conclusion of the general washing rules it is pointed out that such routines apply to all women, young and old, married or single, virgins or prostitutes! Insufficient haphazard care of your perineum can account for years and years of misery. There is no substitute for water, so do not be tempted by any manufactured hygiene aids.

Water is for drinking, and water is for washing.

7. Intercourse

Once again we have no figures on the incidence of sexual cystitis. One can assume that all brides are going to be sore on their honeymoon, but we may also assume that for many, insufficient hygiene is going to advance that soreness into full-blown honeymoon cystitis. It used to be called the bride's disease, the honeymoon disease, and elicited snickering giggles. Doctors would pat the young sufferer on the shoulder and murmur bland reassurances into her ear, perhaps prescribing antibiotics in case of infection.

Your sex drive can dictate how sore you become. Pitching around for hours on end obviously promotes more soreness than half an hour once a day! A doctor once sighed that the sooner honeymoons become redundant and unfashionable, the sooner will brides suffer less. That is all very well, but even if you have plenty of sex before marriage, those two weeks or so with sex as the main idea are still with us. Couples who spend a lot of time apart, suddenly being flung together, will overindulge for hours as though they were on a honeymoon. In truth, just a couple of lengthy sessions following one another swiftly are enough to make both man and woman intensely sore.

Q. Why?
A. Vaginal skin is ten times more sensitive than any other skin on your body.

Q. Why can intercourse cause infection?
A. The woman's bottom, unless previously cleansed, is loaded with potentially harmful germs.

Sexual intercourse accounts for a vast amount of cystitis, but natural reluctance to discuss such attacks with anyone makes a diagnosis very difficult. Amazingly some doctors (but not many fortunately) still don't think the act of sex can cause an attack. Such extreme ignorance is thoroughly disgraceful, particularly when you realize that the bride's disease was common knowledge in the eighteenth and nineteenth centuries.

The missionary position, widely used since man rose onto two legs, is now only one of a multitude of ideas in lovemaking. With widespread and often free contraceptives there is much more intercourse going on and of a varied nature. Sex magazines promote all manner of erotic ideas, some of which can actually be hazardous and all of which are intended to increase sexual appetites. Few people seem to realize just how youthful people were when their sex lives began centuries ago. The first sign of menstruation meant adulthood. Marriage followed, and so did babies; but the constant reminders of sex were not blasting out of radios, stereos, television sets, and films or leering at us from billboards and journals.

Women's bodies didn't have to take the kind of regular vaginal battering that they do today.

This, of course, doesn't mean women don't enjoy it. On the contrary, they actually seek it. When they don't get sex for long periods of time, depression starts. Much middle-age depression is due to the cessation—for whatever reason—of intercourse.

Only when one fails to have sex for a long while is it possible to realize how very important this act is for good mental health. In some enlightened mental homes sex between inmates is regarded as good quieting therapy. I know of one mixed home where troublesome women or girls, if caught in compromising situations, were put on the Pill, made "safe," and allowed to have sex with the chosen male partner. Marked reductions in ward troubles resulted, and the partners were given a quiet room for an hour or so in which to relieve emotions and frustrations with dignity.

As food is to the stomach so sex is to the mind—having it often and when you want it is a worthy aim. Keeping yourself "available" for that amount of intercourse involves caring for your vagina.

Some gynecologists, for want of better advice to give, will tell a cystitis patient to "give it up" for six months. Unbelievable! Simple logic guarantees that the advice won't work—sex may not be the cause of the cystitis at all. But if it is, when the six months are up the attacks will start again.

Within the simple act of intercourse lie many health pitfalls, many future sex stoppers, many cystitis aggravants. Once you know them you can prevent them from ruining your sex life and you can be available for several sessions a day until your stamina wears out.

CONTRACEPTIVES

Before you begin any act of intercourse other than that intended to make a baby, you will be choosing a contraceptive. Choice also depends on what is suitable and painfree for your body. If you decide to use the Pill, and your legs, breasts, and body swell up unbearably and won't go down over a couple of months, it probably isn't suiting your hormone balance. Headaches and the first-time-ever appearance of vaginitis are also capable of making you change your mind. Should the Pill start yeast and vaginitis, give it up—they will stop you from having sex, thus making the whole idea of contraception unnecessary. See if another kind suits you better, as it did this woman:

> "I am twenty-nine years old and have had cystitis off and on for six and a half years. As I have been on the Pill for six of those years, it was a long time before it occurred to me that there might be a connection. Just over a month ago I changed my Pill for a mini-Pill which my doctor was testing on some patients. Since then my soreness has practically vanished, and wine and sex this month have not had their usual disappointing outcomes."

Spermicidal creams may cause problems, too. They aren't particularly a delight to use in the middle of foreplay, but since your partner probably won't like his fingers scooping out frothy cream there's no help except to insert just before he penetrates. Spermicidal cream can cause allergic or irritant reactions in the vagina. It can do the same for the tip of the male penis. Inflammation in the vagina from the cream is worsened with the penile pounding which your cervix is taking. The vagina will probably sting a little anyway after intercourse in normal women using such cream, but in a cystitis-prone woman the stinging will increase until the whole vagina and perineum feel on fire! Cold water helps, but it may not counteract the chemical reaction still working on the skin deep inside. Soon the urethra is involved, particularly if particles of cream have been introduced into it during intercourse. Within hours your urethra and bladder are on fire as well, and besides applying a great many cold water compresses to the perineum, you must employ the entire self-help management process of dealing with an attack. This is maybe one occasion when a cool-water douche could be helpful, but since you are now warned, such a trigger attack can obviously be avoided!

"Five years ago my first attack of cystitis seemed to correspond with the use of a chemical contraceptive called Staycept and sold widely in family planning units in England. All tests and X rays were negative, bicarbonate helped the pain sometimes, but intercourse always aggravated it. At the time I suggested that my cystitis might be caused by the use of this pessary but was told the idea was 'nonsense.' This was repeated on several occasions. Unfortunately since the birth of my twins I have had various problems with mechanical devices and the Pill and had settled for this pessary, so I persevered. However, as an experiment sometime later I stopped using Staycept and substituted another pessary, which my husband didn't like. After several weeks my symptoms of pain and cystitis became milder, and my family planning doctor confirmed eventually that I was allergic to Staycept and probably other chemicals as well. My husband finally solved our problem altogether by having a vasectomy, but the doctor did add that an allergy such as mine could take five months to subside after the final pessary. Recently I met a woman who had cystitis for ten years. One day she gave up her chemical contraceptive, substituted the Pill, and has had no further trouble."

The effects of contraceptives are variable in each woman. Here is another history:

"We have always used contraceptive pessaries, which have never let us down in twenty-three years of marriage, but after more frequent attacks of unexplained and investigated cystitis, also a course of Valium, the hospital said there was nothing to be found. By then I was becoming a little suspicious that I was now allergic to the pessaries or indeed to my husband's semen as it seemed odd that my attacks had worsened after my husband's operation for hydrocele. We discussed how we could find out and began to use a condom. This we have done for six months now with no attacks except one when we reverted to the pessaries to see what would happen. So there we are: I'm allergic either to pessaries or to my husband!"

Another woman got cystitis after her husband's vasectomy; but it would be a brave attempt to theorize on this, and it was the only such case reported to the author's knowledge.

More women have had a rubber allergy to the condom; but there have not been many, and there could have been other undiscovered factors. The condom these days isn't always a straightforward affair. There are exotic colors and "extrasensory" protuberances spiked all over the surface. If you like them and they don't upset your vagina, keep using them. Remember the best rule of all is: If it's comfortable with no ill effect, it's all right for me.

Mechanical contraceptives, such as the old diaphragm, or Dutch cap, or the more modern IUD (intrauterine device), have caused trouble as well. The broad firm rim of the Dutch cap can be buffeted against the cervix and high vagina during intercourse. Forgetting to take it out can precipitate infections as well as cause pressure on the adjoining bladder during the act of intercourse. The coil (IUD) has to be inserted by a trained family planning doctor. Some coils become slightly kinked, twisted, or bent on insertion and cause dull, nagging pain thereafter. Often such an accident is visible only after removal by a very trained eye, but the tiniest kink in the coil would be likely to press somewhere that it shouldn't. Women who have had trouble in childbirth are often regarded as unsuitable candidates for the IUD because of scars and injuries. There is a substantial rise in infections of the uterus and cervix in women wearing IUDs. Watch out!

If cystitis or permanent feelings of soreness appear to you to coincide with the commencement of a new form of contraceptive, regard it seriously. Experiment if possible by stopping and then starting again with the suspect, but if it is the Pill, remember its effects can last for many months. Low-dosage Pills are preferable for all sensitive women and include any one of the varieties claiming thirty to seventy-five milligrams of estrogen.

Sterilization is a relatively recent advent in contraception, but pelvic congestion is becoming recognized as a side effect when blood and rejected cells cannot get past the looping of the Fallopian tubes. Pressure tends to build up, and unexplained pains follow, with sex becoming uncomfortable; sometimes there is bladder involvement as well.

All women must now accustom themselves to the idea of changing or having to change contraceptives several times in their lives. From your late thirties or after the final baby it is perhaps a good idea for your partner to have a vasectomy. Some doctors won't agree—they are mostly men, though! With the woman having done her best for fifteen or twenty years to provide contraceptive help and the problems of childbearing in addition, it really doesn't seem much to ask the man to spend a day in the hospital or have a lunch-hour vasectomy. He will be sore for about ten days, but so were you—and for longer after your babies!

So contraceptive rules are:

- If it's comfortable and you are healthy, use it.
- If you develop strange aches and pains coincidentally, check it out.
- If it hurts, change it.

Now that you have been warned of possible contraceptive triggers of cystitis, we can turn attention to the sex act itself.

COPING WITH INTERCOURSE

All women "know" when they have just had intercourse. The vagina feels hot and often swollen. The inner labia swell quite a lot, become very dark red, and are tender to touch. The perineum feels very wet and sticky, but you feel terrific! It is at this early stage after intercourse that you can do most to prevent an attack of cystitis. What you do or don't do now a quarter of an hour after your partner has withdrawn can decide whether you will be fit for another sexual session tomorrow or you'll be heading for the doctor.

The swollen outer labia are indicative of a similar state inside you and you must reduce the swelling. If you don't, any minute crack or injury in your battered vagina will harbor one or more of the multiple germs now swimming around your perineum. This swelling is called bruising and trauma (shock), and needs that incredibly cheap and simple product called water to wash it down and cool it off.

Cool or even cold water used as in the washing chapter is vital in aiding the vagina and perineum to reduce their size. If you run cool water from a bottle over your perineum now, it enables you to wash a little inside the vagina as well. Gently cleanse the entire area with your free hand as the water is running over the skin. Stop for a minute, and pass urine to flush out the urethra. It may sting a little, but that doesn't matter because if you don't, the urethra will keep any invading germs to itself for some time and the stinging will later be much worse. Flush out the urethra, and then drink a quick glass of water to replace the lost urine.

Much store is put on lying in bed in the euphoria of *après sex* by women's magazines, and for ordinary women that's fine. Not for sufferers of cystitis, though.

The minimum *après sex* care is to pass water and to wash as described.

When this is accomplished, go rest. Since most intercourse happens at night, bed rest follows automatically, but if it occurs in the day, don't put your clothes on and go for a walk; sit or lie without underwear, and give your perineum as much cooling air as possible. Remember the old street story of brides going around without underwear? Why don't you?

Indoors there's no reason why you should not, and it will help your vaginal skin to calm down. Every act of intercourse, whether it is with or without orgasm, requires this cooling-down precedure, and at whatever time of the day or night it occurs. If it's one in the morning, crawl out of bed, pass urine, drink a glass of water, and wash. It pays dividends.

Now that you have learned how to combat bruising and subsequent infection, there are other things to do and be aware of before and actually during intercourse.

The washing procedure previously given is a must. If you have flown home from the office to get supper and tidy up, your partner might have arrived home earlier than usual. Spontaneity is quite OK, but mutter that you are bursting and won't be a second. Back shortly! Pass water if your bladder is uncomfortable, and wash quickly with a bottle of cool water. Thirty seconds or even a minute are all that both these procedures involve. He won't notice—he's too busy arranging himself. After that you are better off than you were.

If intercourse is otherwise more relaxed a procedure, as in bed each night, more things have to be thought out beforehand in appraisal of your cystitis.

A full bladder and a full bowel provide barriers of some solidarity against which a fully erect penis can push. With the vagina sandwiched between the bladder at the front and the rectum behind full of feces, it can hardly escape a battering. What sometimes makes it even more painful is the lowered cervix, before and during a period. Under such conditions there is virtually no room for anything in your vagina, let alone a rampant male.

Make sure your bowels open every day if you are sexually active. Get this procedure out of the way at an inconspicuous time of the day, and then relax about it. You may have to empty your bladder before sex if it feels tingly or full. Try to have just a little urine for passing after intercourse, and always excuse yourself for a quick visit to the bathroom in the middle of a lengthy sex session if you feel uncomfortable. If you are too shy to do this, don't be; otherwise, you will find it impossible to climax normally with tense muscles.

If you have been drinking alcohol before sex, your bladder may be in the middle of the excitement phase of excreting. A lot of alcohol and a lot of sex with no intermixed bland liquid can start an attack of cystitis twelve to fifteen hours later. If you have been that careless, laugh and remember the enjoyment of it all; but put the kettle on for a hot-water bottle, and drink at least a couple of pints of water straight on the first urethral signals. *Don't* neglect those signals!

Having intercourse during a period was absolutely forbidden centuries ago, and many religions still forbid it. They do so with good reason. Blood is the ideal home for germs; in fact, the two-and-a-half-day culture in a laboratory grows bacteria in blood and glucose. Your menstrual blood is no different. However, with careful hygiene, a gentle male, and plenty of towels there is no reason to desist if you simply can't. Intercourse must be played gently and slowly, though. The cervix is heavy with the gathered blood, and the process of the passage of blood directly out of the uterus means that "up there" is very sensitive. Signal if it hurts, and unless he's one of the few men who consciously cause pain, he will slow down and be more accommodating.

So we progress to things modern. Anal intercourse is not that modern, but more of it is being practiced in response to pornography. Anal intercourse may be enjoyable, but it is totally hazardous to health. On the basis of what you have read so far in this book you will well know that the bowels contain millions of germs. Since girlie magazines won't spell it out for fear of falling sales, this book will. Fecal matter on a penis which is inserted into your vagina is filthy. Such action will give you an enormous and acutely embarrassing vaginal infection. You will be unable to have intercourse for several weeks and could be very ill if you are too shy to seek medical help. If you must have anal intercourse, try to have emptied your bowels earlier as a precaution and absolutely insist on the use of a condom. It must be immediately discarded upon withdrawal from the anus and intercourse stopped entirely for a short moment in order to wash hands and scrub under fingernails—his particularly—and to wash the perineum with a little soap in the anal region as well.

Deep and hard vaginal penetration can bruise and injure the cervix. Scars from childbirth can tighten when relaxing would be better during intercourse. If you have any regularly sore area in your vagina, ask a gynecologist to check carefully and give advice. If nothing surgical can be achieved, then you and your partner must choose positions in which the direct pushing bypasses the sore patch. Experiment, and don't hesitate to signal pain of an unusual or distinct nature.

Vibrators are also modern. They should be

washed very carefully, if not actually sterilized, and should be stored in a frequently washed plastic bag or holder. Care should be taken not to scrape your vaginal skin or to grind the cervix to a pulp!

Oral sex has gained an increasing number of fans. The doctor sees more men and women with herpes, mouth and throat infections and oral fungus. Some sexual infections can be spread by oral/genital contact, and VD units will nowadays inquire if oral sex has recently taken place. Herpes has as yet no known cause or cure. It is a virus and contagious— spread by contact with one of its sores. One school of thought, so far unproved, says that chemicals in the vagina can slightly alter in composition when mixed with saliva. Should a tongue or mouth contact the vagina the virus may be formed. After that it can be spread by future oral/genital contact. Herpes is either on the mouth and nose or in the genital organs of both sexes. Don't touch anyone with a mouth sore, and ask discreetly about your prospective partner's sexual health. If in doubt, the condom must be used.

It is not always possible to be lubricated enough to permit penile penetration. If penetration is attempted into a dry, closed-up vagina, the skin will nick and split minutely. This not only gives rise to increasing soreness during sex but also gives easy access for germs into the injured tissues.

Keep a tube of jelly by Johnson & Johnson by the bed. Use it as necessary in either a smear or absolute dollops all over you and him. It has no allergic properties, no harmful chemicals, and is absolutely sterile and nonirritant. It is obtained at any drugstore without prescription and is a unique intercourse aid which can be used before and during long intercourse. Men love it, and it releases you from "I'm too tired!" As a result, you relax immediately and are soon drawn into the prevailing mood. It is, however, only useful to patients during intercourse or when inserting tampons, and won't help during the day if you feel sore for any other reason.

A woman with a sinus infection involved in an act of oral sex is not the healthiest of women to make love to; neither is a man with candida/monilia in his penis the best person to do a "deep throat" with. Candida of the female throat is seen in the doctor's office, and the doctor knows why! With more intercourse occurring in this generation and ingenuity of positions growing in all sorts of couples, continuance of enjoyment must be ensured. It isn't necessary to be ill afterward, provided you understand that germs are always present. Reduce their activity level, and you can increase yours.

Instructions so far in this chapter have been specifically for the woman, but what a male partner does or does not practice is equally important. He can cause cystitis and soreness in his partner, giving years of distress, unless he is made aware of his role. One man wrote me:

> "One thing that surprised me about your television program was that you were overkind to husbands. Few husbands bother about such details as careful washing prior to sex; they are almost invariably too preoccupied with the excitement of the situation and are almost certainly lulled by liberal doses of beer, whiskey, etc. No book on sex that I can find indicates the importance of male hygiene, but I am convinced that I added greatly for years to my wife's cystitis. Apart from sex, few men are fastidious about their underwear and the very nature of their suits,

etc., is such that they rarely spend money on cleaning. The whole setup in civilized man's mode of life makes him a positive cause of cystitis. I am 100 percent sincere in my beliefs and very anxious to make amends for the pain and suffering caused to my very dear and uncomplaining wife over so many years."

This man and many more would willingly cooperate in helping their wives if they knew what to do. Men with urinary problems have a chapter to themselves, but since we are dealing with preventing sexually triggered cystitis in this chapter, this last section will be on dos and don'ts for male partners.

Most important of all for a man is to eradicate, reduce, or recognize possible areas of infection which may be passed to his female partner.

If you are not circumcised, make sure your foreskin is retractable. Never skip an opportunity to retract and cleanse. If you bathe every day, you are passable! It would certainly help further if you gave your penis a quick once-over before making love, particularly if you have been hot and sweaty all day in buses, trains, planes, and offices. If you don't bathe each day, then washing before intercourse is fully as important as your partner's washing. If you cannot retract your foreskin and your partner's onset of cystitis coincided with the first time you both made love and on nearly all subsequent occasions, go straight to a doctor. Ask nicely, demand, beg, change doctors, anything, but get circumcised! The chances are very strong that you are causing her cystitis, and the attacks will impede your joint sexual adventures.

Are your hands and fingers in a good state? This depends on your job. Your hands and particularly your fingers play the initial and important role in lovemaking. Stimulating your partner's clitoris, labia, and vagina with rough fingers is not going to relax her. Instead, she will go tense on you, waiting for the next movement to see if it pains her. What your job does to your hands could be at the root of her attacks of cystitis.

Working on a building site means that every day you return home with broken fingernails—file them smooth before you make love. Unless you carefully scrub and rinse your hands, they will harbor minute particles of building dust, which will irritate her vagina dreadfully. The same goes for demolition workers!

Any rough work which callouses the hands and breaks the nails can nick, injure, bruise, or rub your partner's highly sensitive vagina.

Office workers tend to have long fingernails. To provide maximum help and comfort to the female sex partner, all fingernails should be below the tip of your finger. If they are above, they can only cause trouble.

Do you work in chemicals? If chemicals of any sort—dyes, sprays, paints, photographic chemicals—touch your hands at all, let alone daily, scrub and rinse them several times when you return home. Perhaps some skintight protective gloves at work would eliminate worries like this.

When you stimulate your partner, smear some of her jelly on your finger if she is too dry, and stroke her. Don't press hard unless she's really tough. If she has had a baby, she may have stitch scars or even the scar from the episiotomy, running along her perineum from the vagina, which the surgeon cut to let the baby's head out more easily. That scar is always tender, so try to avoid it or it might split a little and provide a good entrance for germs.

If you touch her anus or even penetrate it slightly, don't use that finger again on her. Sticking it straight into her vagina could cause an *E. coli* infection which will put a stop to intercourse for a couple of weeks.

Herpes was mentioned a little earlier, but it's worth a mention to you. Mouth sores will be passed not only onto her lips but also to her perineum and vagina if you use oral love play. If nothing like that ever affects you or your partner, carry on, but if it does, here is a possible reason why it does.

Watch all her signals during sex. If she falters, draws back, says "ouch," or "I'd rather not," or "no," to something you are doing, respect her. She knows what her vagina feels like, and it differs each time. For instance, she won't want a knees-up position or deep penetration near a period. Use her moods to suit your thrills. Change positions several times in lovemaking so that no single area of her vagina is constantly rubbed and the pressures are evenly spread.

Initial penetration should not be attempted unless your partner is wet enough and relaxed enough. If she is in difficulty because of a long day or some strain, use masses of jelly, and go in slowly and carefully. You will feel her open up and give in to you as the minutes go by, but if she doesn't always respond, just replenish the jelly and do your best.

All this will prevent bruising and give her pain-free intercourse but, more important, it will enable you to make love to her again and again without fear of an attack of cystitis.

"My husband and I thought the sex routines you advocated a little excessive, so we tried to cut corners; but since my last attack in December, we have come to our senses, and now for the first time in six years of marriage we can enjoy intercourse with no worries. To think we suffered all the agonies for six years when the solution was such a thing as simple hygiene. We are not dirty, of course, but until you get problems, it doesn't occur to you to wash before and after sex. I feel family planning units should give simple warnings and hygiene instruction while they fit devices or prescribe contraceptives."

8. Men

Men have troubles with their bladder and urethra. Of that there is no doubt, but at this point such troubles do not take on the proportions of those from which women suffer. The medical profession does not term such troubles cystitis but more commonly divides symptoms under the following headings:

- Prostatitis: inflammation of the prostate gland
- Urethritis: inflammation of the urethra
- Nonspecific urethritis: inflammation of unrecognized origin.

After these casual names most other illnesses associated with bladder, kidneys, ureters, and so on usually appear with the same names as those in women—i.e., stones, pyelitis.

Men suffer in one way far worse than women do. Any woman who's been pregnant is used to the intimate medical examination, and when you've had it once, it's not too bad at all. Men, though, never have this unless something is wrong with their penises, testicles, or bladders, and they seldom disclose such highly personal problems to a friend, or very often to their wives.

"I am sixty years of age now, and when I was forty-eight years of age, with terrible suddenness, one Saturday evening in August of that year 'it' struck me in all its ferocity and completely altered the course of my working, domestic, and social life. I had two attacks of pyelitis in three weeks, rigors, temperature 104.5, passing blood, with excruciating pain, and all the symptoms of a long road to recovery, aching limbs, etc., etc.

"Since then at intervals (fewer attacks), terrible frequency, no pain, no blood, etc., just frequency, which can be ten to twelve hours a day, every day, and, as in the present attack, lasting nineteen months and still going strong. The effect is demoralizing, wearing, and degrading to the point of my sometimes being at the far end.

"One carries on at work (luckily my job allows me to visit the toilet whenever I wish; otherwise, in many jobs work at times would have been impossible), but social life is out and in any case devoid of pleasure. Four years after my pyelitis attacks, my wife (age now forty-seven) started an attack of cystitis, frequency, intense pain, but not passing blood, so for some time we were attending the hospital as a dual act, myself at the time being in the middle of terrible frequency, which attack lasted three months.

"Fourteen months back I was cystoscoped in the hospital for the second time (very nasty for a man), but nothing to cause the trouble was discovered. I have had courses of Penbriten, Neg Gram, and the latest idea when they send for me is to go into the hospital and have my bladder distended, cystoscopy again being necessary.

"A feature of my frequency is that on rising in the morning, and for the first four, five, or even sometimes six hours, I am normal; then the trouble creeps on and builds up so that by the evening and bedtime and until I get to sleep, I have pressure every five minutes and need to empty my bladder (two or three ounces), and even in bed I have terrible pressure, sometimes when holding probably no more than a tablespoon of urine; then I am OK.

"It is a cruel complaint, and I very often despair of ever getting rid of the present attack. I observe the rules, no alcohol, coffee, etc. I wonder if you get other letters from men about this trouble.

"Sex life is, of course, 100 percent nil, and only tolerance and understanding hold people together; it is more a question of surviving living than living for any purpose or pleasure, and of course, among people with whom you work or socialize, it is a subject on which they do not wish to hear you airing your misery. I know only one thing: It was a sad day when it walked into my life.

"I am one of those people whom people stare at in amazement when you say you are sixty; people take me for being forty-five to fifty without exception, so I wonder how I would have been if cystitis and pyelitis and in my case now frequency had not caused me depression, weariness, and despair."

Prostatitis, or inflammation of the prostate, is often used to describe infection as well. The prostate gland is situated at the base of the penis, and if any infection reaching it has arrived by way of the long penile urethra, clearing the prostate infection may take some time. Men from the late fifties onward are more likely to have prostate trouble than their younger counterparts. Symptoms are much the same as in true cystitis, but sometimes they can be just frequency of urination.

This kind of frequency in an older man probably results not because he has taken to drinking a bottle of whiskey a day or increased his morning coffee intake to a couple of pints but usually because the prostate gland tends to enlarge at this time of life. In severe frequency, which is almost incontinence, the prostate has enlarged so much that it causes pressure on the increasingly aging and sensitive bladder. The bladder feels full, but very little urine is excreted when the toilet is visited, or the pressure is such that urine constantly dribbles out.

At this stage, surgery is usually performed, after many tests to ensure an accurate diagnosis. When surgery is really necessary, the patient will have an operation called a prostatectomy. As a rule, not all of the gland is removed, only the amount actually impeding the bladder. It takes a month or more to learn how to recontrol the bladder, because one of the two valves controlling the urine mechanism is destroyed, but the remaining one will learn to do the work of its partner if given time.

A diagnosed infection in the prostate not demanding surgery will be treated with antibiotics, but that can take a long while. During and after such drug therapy specialists seldom—in fact, almost never—see fit to understand that men can also suffer from yeast infections. The symptoms of yeast in men are not the same. A man will have a white-coated or furry tongue, he will have a substantial rise in stomach gas, and the intestines and bowels may "grumble." Perhaps the anus will itch, but a penile discharge is not always there as the most obvious symptom.

Antibiotics taken by a man for whatever illness are still likely to cause yeast infection. This in turn

can irritate the urethra and cause burning and stinging.

A woman with a yeast infection can pass it to
her sexual partner, and its symptoms will still be on
the tongue and in the stomach as described. Yeast
can be passed backward and forward between husband and wife until both are diagnosed simultaneously, both treated simultaneously, and both
cleared simultaneously. If you as a man have a sensation of burning when your urine is passing down the
penis, it could be yeast. Go to a genitourinary clinic
or, better still, a VD unit. Here a urine specimen
and a penile swab can ascertain infections of all
sorts, and expert advice is available.

Urethritis is inflammation or infection of the
urethra which runs the length of the penis. With
urine samples and swabs it is possible for a specialist
to diagnose the germ. If you cleanse under the foreskin at least daily, then the chances of your contaminating yourself are practically nil, but not all men
are hygiene-conscious—it is beneath their dignity.
The word "urethritis" is meant as an all-embracing
term. Just because a doctor informs you that you
have urethritis doesn't mean there's anything to
cheer about. He will only give you a broad-spectrum
antibiotic and cross his fingers.

You will become as enlightened as the women
reading this book if you use the self-help management process of dealing with an attack as soon as
you feel unusual sensations in your urethra and bladder. Flushing your kidneys and bladder with plenty
of water at the earliest signals can do nothing but
good and will prevent any rising infections from
going any higher. At the end of three hours your
symptoms probably will have ended, but if you

don't work at it, the infection will rise and almost certainly enter the prostate gland. As with women, self-help is immediately important, and antibiotics later are possibly necessary, though not vital.

In a urology unit recently a young man presented symptoms of increasing frequency. His doctor had tried antibiotics; but these failed (of course, since he showed no symptoms of real infection), and here he was bemoaning his fate to the urologist. The urologist questioned him on some strictly medical facts, but no further light was shed on the mystery. As a couple of tests which the nurse would shortly perform were being explained to him, the young man volunteered that he wondered if stress had anything to do with it, since he had had money worries over house moves when the trouble started. Further questioning revealed he had been drinking more beer after work as a "comfort." His beer drinking had increased considerably, he confessed, and of course, if you drink a lot, you just have to pass it if your bladder is normal! So the young man went away, having wasted twenty valuable minutes of a consultant's time, which might have been better used in dealing with the following case:

> "For the past six and a half years I have suffered intense pain in the groin, testicles, and trunk base. This entire area is always in pain, and intercourse is out. Prior to this I never had any such kind of trouble. Tablets, injections, X rays, and cystoscopies have revealed nothing, not even a psychiatric session later on. My consultant has told me to grin and bear it. I can't grin, and I can't bear it. If nothing is done soon, I'll go out of my mind. My wife and family are marvelous, and my doctor will refer me anywhere that I want to go; but where else can I go?"

When all urological tests appear normal—a second opinion may be requested, though, in a specialty hospital for kidneys—that urologist or someone must come up with other ideas. At such a time one can go off the top of one's head almost into realms of fantasy as to where the source of trouble lies.

Theorizing doesn't hurt at all; but putting theory into practice can, and any experiments must be done through relevant hospital departments. Search the self-help ideas; you may feel some are applicable. Even a man must start at the beginning with: "When did my first attack begin, and were there any unusual circumstances?"

When anyone talks about continuing and unceasing pain—pain, not sensations—and has undergone relevant tests, one casts around for other far-reaching reasons for the pain. Could any kind of spinal injury or back injury, however small, have occurred at the onset of attacks? Pain from such a source can and does inflict radiating pain, upsetting nerve endings over large areas. A trip to the neurology unit may reveal a reason for such inexplicable cases.

Another way-out effort may be made at an acupuncture center. Here the fascinating pulse readings can indicate accurately a malfunctioning organ, and if you locate an acupuncturist with proper medical qualifications as well, you could be in very good care.

With a patient complaining only of frequency and/or urethral sensations self-help for self-induced illness should be investigated. Here are some ideas:

· Your sex partner can obviously infect you with all manner of bacteria. Be careful with whom you sleep. Check her throat for streptococci before you try oral sex.

- Use a condom for anal intercourse, and don't infect your penis with her bowel bacteria.
- Perhaps she uses antiseptic tissues to clean her bottom, and the antiseptic irritates your penis. A lot of women wrongly use vaginal deodorants, which will also irritate your penis.
- Avoid all penile contact with toiletries—i.e., do you wash your hair in the bath and sit in the shampoo bubbles?
- Nylon Y fronts prevent air from keeping the penis and testicles cool. In the resulting moist warmth, fungus infections will start, exacerbated by nylon-mixture trousers and tight blue jeans. The general cleanliness of tight trousers and jeans is suspect, and stale secretions from your visits to the toilet will harbor other bacteria.
- Have your clothes cleaned or washed regularly.
- Change your Y fronts each day, and follow the washing routine recommended in our laundering advice.
- Acidity, diet, and quality of urine mean just the same to a man. If you feel like cutting out all those sugar lumps in your hot drinks, do it.

It is possible to develop allergies to food and drink, which may affect the bladder. Suppose your attacks of burning and frequency coincide with headaches each time. Keep a dossier on all that you ate and drank up to forty-eight hours before the attack. Twenty-four hours may suffice, and three attacks later you could have one or more common factors present in your food and drink before each of those attacks. Narrow them down by cutting them out one at a time, or go to your doctor for allergy reaction tests. The migraine clinic could also be helpful.

If you know that vodka, for instance, makes you spend countless extra hours in the toilet, don't drink it; try something else.

Men test their bladders from the time they come of age to when they die. Please read the alcohol section in Chapter 5 and ask yourself if it is a good thing to give your kidneys an unrelenting supply of coffee and alcohol. Rest up now and again. One man observed:

> "Unfortunately I am plagued by long bouts of prostatitis, with some colitis and urethritis. Dozens of tests have produced no underlying cause for my distress. My consultant has expressed a view that nothing more can be done at present but much research is being done. Meanwhile, I take my sulfadimidine to 'maintain my condition.' I have noticed that when my back gets chilled, an attack seems to start."

The kidneys in men and women react in the same way. As before, the recommendation is to drink a couple of glasses of water or some hot weak beverage to replace the urine excreted in response to hot and cold stimuli.

> "I became ill with my second attack of cystitis last week and feel that at sixty-four years of age more may be on the horizon. During this attack several men have revealed themselves as fellow sufferers, so I feel inclined to know if there is anything I can do to avoid or manage future attacks."

NSU—nonspecific urethritis—is being researched quite closely. Such researchers are hell bent on finding out what it is, what causes it, and why it starts. It is increasing by dint of the numbers of men now attending clinics. The scientists may well find something tangible and exciting, but this author believes that, as with the female urethral syndrome, it doesn't really exist at all and is only an excuse for failing to recognize and diagnose all sorts of obscure causes. For instance, how many specialists or family doctors are going to inquire into all the tiny details of self-induced bladder troubles, such as your girl friend's use of vaginal deodorant or whether you both get a headache at the same time?

Patients become tongue-tied in the face of a white-coated consultant and fail to communicate all their own little homespun theories. Undoubtedly NSU occurs with intercourse, but when all well-known bacteria have been eliminated during investigations, there is still a bacterial substance known as *Chlamydia*. This is apparently highly infectious and not always easy to diagnose, though often it is accompanied by other conditions. Treatment is of around three weeks' duration and involves the female partner as well. *Chlamydia* responds to tetracycline but needs clearance tests in both partners. Sometimes in men there is a throat infection, in women inflammation of the pelvis, and in newborn babies "sticky eye" as indications of chlamydial infection, and spreading it around is achieved not only by intercourse but also occasionally by transference on fingers, facecloths, or towels.

The more women that you have intercourse with, the greater the risk of genital troubles. Use a condom for casual relationships.

Bladder cancer is more common in men than women. Any bleeding from the penis with or without pain should be investigated by a urologist as quickly as possible. It could be only a kidney stone or one of many other less urgent problems, but cancer has to be ruled out. Smokers account for the largest group of bladder cancer patients among men. Smoking does not affect just the lungs since its toxic substances are carried around the body by the bloodstream. Treatment for bladder cancer, if caught early enough, is by cauterization of the tumors at roughly three- to four-month intervals under a general anesthetic. If the cancer is discovered in an advanced stage, it may mean removal of the entire bladder. When will men and women realize that the chewing or smoking of tobacco leaves or any other leaves causes serious body injuries? Stop smoking!

9. Questioners' Forum

Q. Three years ago I had a small duodenal ulcer but have had no trouble since. Do you think that taking bicarbonate of soda even irregularly is safe, and does the same answer apply to painkillers?

A. No, the same answer does not apply to painkillers. The majority of painkillers are acidic, and as most ulcer patients know only too well, food and drink of an acidic nature are to be strongly avoided. Aspirin is not recommended, and the patient should carefully study all packaging for painkillers to see the contents. The pharmacist himself or, of course, your family physician will help you if you feel doubtful.

Bicarbonate of soda is what we call an antacid and should not be a problem. A daily dose of one level teaspoon to reduce excess acidity, or the three level teaspoons in the three hours of the management process are our normal recommendations. Further queries should be addressed to your family physician.

Q. I have a watery discharge from the rectum. Could you tell me the correct type of specialist to see and possibly give me some thoughts as to what this discharge might be? I might mention briefly a past history of mild diverticulosis, hysterectomy, fibroids, and a not terribly helpful doctor.

A. The specialist who deals with bowel disorders or malfunctions is called a proctologist. Under a local anesthetic he will insert a proctoscope—the same sort of idea as a cystoscope—so that he can examine the rectal passage and bowels for any abnormalities such as pus cells, blood, ulcers, tumors, hemorrhoids, and so on. He will take swabs and grow cultures of the organisms within the rectum and bowels and commence treatment according to the swab reports and his own sight findings.

We feel it is imperative with this kind of abnormal rectal discharge that you visit the proctologist immediately. Accuracy is essential, and only careful and quick tests will reveal what might be a difficult case.

Q. For the past eighteen months I have suffered consistently from *E. coli* infections. My last specimen showed that the germ is now sensitive to only three drugs. What will the position be when I am immune to these?

A. First, it is important to know where this *E. coli* is coming from. Presumably, detailed blood tests have been done to ascertain whether the infection is being carried in the blood from the bowels to the bladder. If they have and the results are negative, then the infection is probably of an ascending type, e.g., across the perineum from the rectal orifice.

We suggest that you look very sensitively for flaws along your hygiene system.

We have never yet heard of a patient running out of effective drugs—there always seems to be an alternative somewhere!

Q. What is cervical erosion?

A. Cervical erosion is a condition of the cervix (neck of the womb) and is very common in all age-groups, even babies! It is especially common in women taking the Pill and after pregnancy. If it is described as an ulcer on the cervix, this is incorrect because no ulceration is present.

Erosion is, in fact, caused by the creeping out of the delicate mucus-secreting cells that line the interior cervical opening to form a patch about the size of a quarter on the cervix. By inserting a speculum and having a good view, the doctor sees this patch as a glistening bright red.

Because the cells in this red patch are extra-delicate, unlike the tougher ones which line the outer cervix and the vagina, all the unhealthy, but quite natural, inhabitants of our body seem to find a home in them. Thus, the red patch can end up infected with something or other, and a discharge may then begin.

Cervical erosion can possibly account for unexplained bleeding during the menstrual cycle outside the actual week of menstruation itself. Intercourse may also start it bleeding by dint of bruising or damage.

Treatment for mild erosion is sometimes not even necessary because it can come and go by itself, but if discharge or other symptoms are present, positive help should be given. A cancer smear is simply part of the tests to find out the substance of the red patch and ascertain the best treatment to be given. Cauterization under a general anesthetic is a small five-minute operation and generally does the trick. Cryosurgery, a more modern technique involving the freezing idea rather than the burning away of seats of infection, is usually painfree, unless a deep-seated cervical erosion emanating from the uterus is receiving attention. Then the uterus aches a little in much the same way as a tooth coming to life after dental injections.

Although some gynecologists prefer to leave erosion alone, they really should remove the seat of infection from the cervix if the patient continually complains of irritations and infections of the vagina and perineum.

Q. How can one improve the debilitation and depression after long courses of antibiotics?

A. We presume that a long period of debilitation and depression is due to alteration in the gut flora (the surface of internal tissue abounds with tiny bacteria of all sorts—good, bad, and indifferent) by antibiotics. These pills eradicate most bacterial varieties, leaving a kind of no-man's-land and encouraging growth of hardier germs able to survive this breeding ground. It may take a month or two for the gut to recolonize with the normal bacteria, and while this is happening, one tends to get stomach upsets and presumably a secondary reflection on general health.

Of course, the general toxicity of antibiotics on the central nervous system has been studied, but there is still no scientific evidence available to say that antibiotics may be responsible for depression, although many women may complain of feeling depressed while on a long course.

It is extremely important to maintain a large intake of vitamins, protein, and iron during long courses of antibiotics and for a couple of months afterward. Not just good food but any vitamin capsules and iron pills which your pharmacist might recommend. It's a boring job but very necessary.

Q. Can cystitis run in families?

A. We know of no statistical study that has been done to prove this point. Unless there is any transmittable congenital defect in the urinary tract, we really cannot see that this can occur. It may be possible that whereas children inherit parents' colorings and bodily features, they possibly inherit skin types and with it varying degrees of sensitivity. Patterns of social behavior tend also to be passed down from parent to child—particularly early lessons in hygiene (or the lack of them), the way the perineum is cleaned, or even the use of a favorite bath soap, talcum powder, or deodorant.

On the whole, there is no documented evidence at present to say that cystitis is more prevalent in some families than in others.

Q. I have been married twice. I never had cystitis at all before my second marriage. I'm not going through the change, and I have no children. Why should cystitis start now?

A. We tend to be of the opinion that your husband is either infecting or traumatizing the vagina somehow. The only way to find out the trouble is to ask your husband to go to a genitourinary specialist or unit for a group of tests. If all the tests prove negative, we would suggest that a frank appraisal of the marital relationship be made in consultation with a sympathetic gynecologist.

Q. Could someone tell me why I have to keep sending urine samples to my doctor when the results are always negative? Isn't there some other quick investigation he could do?

A. It is part of modern medical folklore that the doctor wishes to know what is contained in a urine specimen from a woman suffering with cystitis. Two points—both crucial—are usually missed:

1. The most productive specimen is the *first* one passed at the onset of the attack.

2. There must be an immediate culture in a laboratory within two hours.

If it has been established that your urine contains *E. coli* in quantities either large or small, from the point of view of where the *E. coli* is coming from—an unclean perineum constantly contaminating the urethra is the obvious answer—no amount of specimen taking is going to enlighten you or your doctor any further. Sometimes the amount of germs found in the urine is very small, and the laboratory reports "no significant growth." This simply means that there are not sufficient germs to constitute factual, evidential cystitis. Many doctors do consider constant specimens to be a waste of effort, so, after initial reassurance that the urine is not acutely infected regularly, they turn their attention to vaginal swabs.

A quick, painless swab of the cervix and vagina may show up all sorts of conditions, infective or noninfective, which may well have a bearing on the condition of the urethra. There is no reason at all why a family doctor should not perform this simple task. Waiting for a hospital appointment will not catch the problem at its height.

Q. Could someone tell us a little about pain? Why do we have it, and where does it come from?

A. There's an old expression "My nerves are jangling," and that, in a very simplified version, is the explanation. We have to think of the following events in terms of thousandths of a second's timing:

1. Invasion of germ into tissue, or injury.
2. Nerve fiber endings within the tissue also become invaded and damaged.
3. Nerve fiber tells the brain that all is not well.
4. The brain tells nerve fiber to give warning signals of impending trouble.
5. Nerve fiber vibrates and causes pain in the damaged area.

Without this we would not be aware of illness, disease, infections, breakages, and all the other types of problems besetting the body. Pain is a warning—something to be thankful for.

Q. My daughter, aged fourteen years, has simultaneously begun her periods and cystitis. The coincidence is too great. There must be a connection. What is it, please?

A. Obviously one is going to have to explore the reproductive organs for the cause of this particular individual's cystitis. The health and secretions of the vagina affect the urethra and bladder because these organs are closely situated.

A gynecologist would look particularly for signs of the following:

1. Is there any staining on her underwear between periods? This would signify a noneffective leukorrhea, which means excess natural secretions

caused by the new hormone levels involved in menstruation. This excess mucus has no germs but nevertheless can cause irritation on the perineum and in the urethra if it progresses to this organ. Cystitis will follow in the susceptible female. It may in time—say, six months to one year—settle down to a more normal level, or it may not and would need further investigation. Self-help can prevent the cystitis from being a secondary symptom; just wash the mucus away gently and frequently four or five times a day.

2. It may be a yeast infection or some other type of discharge brought on by the youngster's inefficient adult female hygiene. She must be taught that germs thrive in blood, and there's a lot of that around during menstruation. A good cleanup on the sixth day will help. Hot baths will not help.

3. The different menstrual hormones may be making her urine too acid. Litmus-paper checks should be made.

4. It may be caused by improper use of tampons or sanitary pads. Are they being changed often enough, or are they causing any irritation?

5. Has the girl, unknown to you, started to use an intimate deodorant or deodorizing powder on sanitary napkins as so widely, and unfortunately, advertised in women's magazines?

Check exactly when the attacks begin on a three-month chart, and if a pattern occurs, your doctor or gynecologist should be able to help further.

Q. I understand that sexual positions may have some influence on an attack of cystitis. How and why?

A. Remember that the bladder and uterus, urethra, and vagina are separated from each other only by layers of tissue. To illustrate, often, in pregnancy or later in actual labor, the mother-to-be finds it difficult to get urine out. Indeed, in labor it is often impossible to pass water at all because the baby is obstructing the bladder and urethra.

In intercourse, not only are the nerve endings in all these organs rubbed, but slight injury or bruising of the tissue or skin may occur. Some sexual positions will aggravate this still further. Any such position held for a longish time causes more strain on the particular side of the vagina taking the movement, just as using one arm to clean windows all morning may make the arm ache. Use the vagina comprehensively.

A good gynecologist can also tell whether deep penetration of the vagina by the penis happens frequently. If the cervix at the top of the vagina is frequently pummeled about, it's going to get sore, as is the bladder situated approximately at this point. Individual experiment by each couple and reaction by the woman during intercourse to any soreness or sore spots within her vagina, plus a careful and thoughtful use of this sensitive organ, may reduce cystitis related to intercourse.

Q. Can nuns get cystitis?
A. Yes, most definitely. Although, like children, they can forget about sexual causes of cystitis, they still have reproductive organs which can cause hormone problems, discharges, and so forth.

Q. Could you please tell me whether antibiotics are dangerous or even addictive if used often?
A. All antibiotics are dangerous if used without

proper safeguards and proper supervision. It is very unwise for patients to take self-administered drugs without good medical direction until you become a thoroughly trustworthy patient in the doctor's eyes. We think it unwise to have loose antibiotics around the house unless you have a highly sympathetic doctor who is available on the telephone fairly easily or who gives instructions for the use of your antibiotic at the onset of your next attack.

Let me repeat that antibiotics are dangerous when overused and can have unpleasant side effects, some of which can cause yeast infections, thus prolonging an attack of urinary infection. They are certainly not addictive, but over a long course of some months' duration it is possible for the effects of the drug to wear off.

Q. Can cystitis be caused by VD and, when the VD is cured, the cystitis remain?

A. Yes. The process of infecting the bladder lining by VD germs over a long period of time does cause inevitable wear on the tissues of the bladder. They become raw and tender, and the passing of urine over these raw areas will produce discomfort and even pain. The actual germs may have long since been killed, but the damage done to muscles and tissue will remain. Healing sometimes takes more than six months. It is advisable to have the urine checked for bacteria each month, and needless to say, the havoc would not have occurred had the patient sought the help of a VD clinic much earlier or been choosy about her partner.

Q. My daughter is only four years old but already has quite a history of urinary tract infection, asthma, and colds. Am I right in thinking that these

ailments in childhood are connected, and would she perhaps benefit from removal of tonsils and adenoids?

A. Long-standing acute infections in the body are likely to find their way to other points where the germs may show up as something else, e.g., boils. There is some circumstantial evidence to show that there is a secondary connection with UTI—urinary tract infection—but as is the case with so much else in this field of medicine, no one has actually got down to proving it yet. You may well find an improvement in your daughter's condition after tonsils and adenoids have been removed. A food allergy could be responsible.

Q. I never had any trouble at all with my bladder until a cervical smear was taken some months ago, and now I get fairly regular attacks of cystitis. All tests have proved negative, but I am still rather sore. Is there any explanation?

A. It is almost impossible to tell without a detailed cervical examination, but we find it a very unusual case. Cervical smears are taken with a wooden spatula which is just turned around the cervix to gather some of its contents for microscopic examination. Bruising might have temporarily occurred; but this would not cause a recurrence of attacks, and in any case the vagina and cervix are very tough elastic pieces of apparatus.

Q. Aspirin and its associate products are not really very good painkillers for cystitis patients to use, are they? Can you tell us why and suggest alternatives?

A. It is not so much aspirin which is the problem but an ingredient called phenacetin. The trouble is that most analgesics contain phenacetin, and it is this, when taken frequently, that can cause kidney poisoning. It first affects the medulla, which is the top section of each kidney, and the poison damages the very sensitive tissues there, spreading eventually to the main body of the kidney. There is increasing medical evidence that painkillers taken in regular large doses are causing kidney poisoning, and it is advisable for anyone requiring regular painkillers to consult a competent GP and report any feelings of nausea, sickness, or dizziness. For the pain which occurs during an actual attack of cystitis, the bicarbonate decreases the acidity of the urine that is flowing out over the inflamed area. This is an enormous help. On top of this we recommend a couple of capsules of extra-strength Tylenol.

Q. Can you tell us a little about bladder washouts?

A. First they are used only in very severe cases of bladder infection in which encrustation of the bladder lining has taken place. In other words, the crystal content of the urine has been high and has tended to remain on the bladder wall without being passed out through the urethra. This process takes many years and is not particularly common. One other reason for use of a washout is carcinoma, or cancer, of the bladder in which a washout can be soothing and helpful.

It can be performed without a general anesthetic and in a well-protected bed. A tiny catheter is inserted into the urethra and carefully pushed into the bladder. Through the tube flows a somewhat strong antiseptic solution of warm water, which irrigates the bladder and enfolds the impurities. It can then either be allowed to trickle out at its own rate or be drawn or pushed out through the same catheter. Depending on the reason for doing it, it can be used at will either daily or weekly, and the process takes about half an hour in all. The easiest way, of course, to bladder-wash is to drink a lot of water and make sure you pass a lot.

Q. Can we have a little information on aspects of kidney failure?

A. It's a very strange phenomenon that some fatal illnesses become apparent to both doctor and patient only when the disease is so far advanced as to be rendered hopeless. Most of the symptoms we are now going to describe can be attributed to a multitude of illnesses, and many are extremely simple to remedy, so please do not jump to unnecessarily depressing conclusions.

For a start, we all feel tired occasionally, and most women walk around with mild or moderate anemia anyway. Both of these, together with breathlessness, nausea, and the passing of exceptionally large amounts of urine, can be indicative of kidney failure. When these symptoms become severe, the urologist to whom the patient should have been referred will ask for a series of chemical tests on the urine and blood. When these tests show a high blood urea and strong evidence of accumulation of breakdown products of protein and acids, it may be advisable to have renal dialysis. In other words, an artificial machine will cleanse the bloodstream of impurities which the kidneys are failing to eliminate. From here and according to each individual patient, the one or both faulty kidneys can nowadays be removed, and a donor's kidney transplanted.

Q. Is it possible to tell straightaway from a urine specimen whether cancer is present or not?

A. The urine culture which is done from a new patient's first specimen is not designed to show cancer cells. Its purpose is to itemize a great many foreign bodies, such as blood, bacteria, acids, and sugar. Generally an abnormal amount of blood corpuscles, both red and white, should call immediately for further tests, particularly if the patient continually passes blood with each visit to the toilet over a period of time. The GP should not hesitate to take immediate action on these tests, and if cancer is proved to be present, a urologist should be consulted immediately. It is possible nowadays for the cancerous bladder to be removed and an ileostomy performed, and over a year or so the patient can take up the threads of living once more. It is certainly possible now for the cancer to be diagnosed early enough for radium treatment alone to be successful, without surgical intervention. Discussion of cancer these days is easier, thanks to media exposure and medical knowledge, and many cancers can be managed without major surgery. There is less to fear nowadays if the diagnosis is made as early as possible and the treatment begun immediately.

Q. Diabetes affects the bladder, so I'm told. How?

A. Diabetes, in fact, affects the whole body. Its presence is proved by blood and urine tests which disclose a very high level of glucose. The patient, if not treated with insulin, can pass into a coma.

As regards the bladder it can have strange, contradictory symptoms. In some patients incontinence occurs because the bladder nerve endings become useless and damaged, thus leaving the bladder with no stimulus to expel or withhold its urine. It just runs out with little or no control. Likewise the with-holding can cause water retention.

Usually the patient is very thirsty because of the large volumes of water expelled.

Sugar levels in the vagina are higher, and with the accompanying lower level of general health and lower resistance to infections, the likelihood of yeast infection is ever-present. Yeast, as we all know, pre-disposes very heavily toward cystitis. So the diabetic urinary patient is troubled in both the bladder and the vagina.

Q. I always get an attack of cystitis after my period. Is this common, and what can I do about it?

A. Cystitis before or after menstruation is common—very common—and is indicative of a number of causes. If it occurs before a period, or in the menopausal woman at the estimated prearrival time (because cycles still occur in shadow), it is generally heralded with a few twinges and is symptomatic of the buildup of hormones which lead to the breakup of blood and tissue in the uterus, resulting in the actual menstruation. The woman who keeps exceptionally clean at this time is helping herself a lot, particularly if her underwear is cotton and boiled and she washes the perineum several times a day. Just in case the twinges seem to progress quickly to affecting the urethra, it is also useful to watch the drinking, so that a fair amount of dilute urine keeps the bladder clean and the urethra well washed out. Advice from a gynecologist would also help because a short oral course of hormone treatment could go a long way toward increasing vaginal comfort.

For those who appear to get the attack after a

period, it is most beneficial and sensible to have a real cleanup. Coliform from the bowel breeds very well in a blood medium as well as in acidic urine! So wash very frequently, and try using a simple warm-water douche at the end of the period to clear out any remaining stale fluid from the vagina. Tampons don't really help the situation. They can be rough, drying, and an internal irritant. Far better to see that your flow is of normal small volume and of a short period of time so that sanitary pads can be used in comfort. Also, do as the Orthodox Jews advocate, and have no intercourse for the seven days until you have cleaned up.

Q. What is a floating kidney? Is it a serious condition, and can it be rectified?

A. Many people with normal kidneys have remarkable kidney mobility! These two organs may move up or down to a limit of four inches in accordance with respiration. It is very difficult to know whether there is a border line between patients with very mobile kidneys who get symptoms of kidney pain and those who do not. There is a definite, although very small, group of patients who do have very mobile kidneys that descend right down into the pelvis and cause pain. They respond to surgery, which takes the form of stitching the kidneys back up into their rightful position. This operation is called nephropexy.

The kidneys can move independently of each other, and because they appear mobile, there is still no suggestion of anything else's being wrong with them. The condition can be discovered easily enough in the usual IVP kidney X ray if the patient is requested to stand up so that the specialist can see whether the kidney begins a descent.

Q. What is colitis, and in what ways may a patient help toward successful treatment?

A. Colitis is a disease of the colon and may be due to infections caused by abnormal organisms which are not usually found there, or it can be due to another condition called ulcerative colitis, for which the cause is not yet known. There are various groups of colitic conditions, and it may take a little while for accurate diagnosis to be given. But they all mostly bring on symptoms of urinary tract infection. As with all forms of urinary infections the best treatment is prevention, and thus steps should be taken to treat colitis successfully once it has been diagnosed. The most obvious symptom of colitis is diarrhea. If this is persistent and frequent, then the family doctor must refer the patient to a competent gastroenterologist as a first step. This specialist will then take action to discover what is causing the diarrhea, and treatment will commence, depending on his judgments.

The patient can certainly help prevent the urinary infections by simply being extra-fastidious about personal hygiene, e.g., using toilet tissue from the front to the back; washing after defecation, and observing strict hand hygiene as well. Dr. Crook's book, *Are You Allergic?*, may again provide thoughts on a food allergy. For example, daily garlic or onions may irritate the colon; maybe eggs, bran, wheat, and so on.

The patient with colitis will probably become thin because the intestines work so fast in breaking down the food products from the stomach that they have no chance to be absorbed properly into the bloodstream, and so they pass into the bowel as extraneous matter much faster than usual.

Medical treatment is very diffuse for colitis, particularly for ulcerative colitis, which is probably the largest and most important group for which the etiology is not known. There are all sorts of treatments—steroids and sulfonamides, to name but two. It depends on the particular specialist and what he thinks is best.

Q. My daughter, aged eight-and-a-half years, has cloudy, offensive urine and a small vaginal discharge. Our doctor says that she will probably grow out of it, but I am still worried as her schooling is being affected. What further steps can I take to be sure of correcting the problem?

A. "If in doubt, go find out." A good motto for all of us, but particularly so in the case of children's ailments. You are in charge for some years of another human's welfare, and until such time as that human being takes on the job of caring for herself, you as the parent must be held responsible. Like any other illness, urinary infection has degrees of severity, varying from "nothing to worry about" to "kidney deformities begun while the child was in embryo." With a specialist's help you must ascertain the cause of your child's symptoms. Your doctor may indeed be correct, but he should respect your worry and refer you to a urologist, whose second opinion will help set your mind at rest.

Much can be done now for children, provided the mother recognizes the small abnormalities early in the growth of the child. One can endlessly list symptoms, but the most important are observed as part of the child's general health. For instance, listlessness, loss of appetite, frequency of bladder action, unusually small amount of urine passed, cloudy urine, blood streaks in the urine, pain, reddening of urethral area, vaginal discharge—there are as many symptoms as causes.

Observe your child for a few days, and make careful notes of each unusual incident. You will then have evidence of your problem, and this will considerably aid your doctor in a quicker diagnosis.

Q. My urologist says that the ache in my back could be due to something vaginal. Yeast has recently been successfully treated, with resulting freedom from urinary discomfort, but the urge to pass water is still there.

A. First we trust that the urologist has done all necessary in the way of X rays, blood, and urine tests in order to eliminate kidney infection as a cause. Having eliminated this aspect of inquiry, we are left with two others:

1. Spinal investigations, possibly with a neurological survey.

2. Gynecological investigations of the uterus, cervix, and vagina.

The nerve impulses which come from the brain through your spine to the bladder are control signals telling your bladder that it is full and needs to be emptied. If these signals are disrupted by either injury or disease, the bladder is in trouble. Either it won't work at all or it works nonstop with all the variations in between, according to the mildness or severity of the original injury or disease. The back, of course, will ache, and the bladder will misbehave.

The uterus is held in place by ligaments, which provide the surrounding muscles with extra strength; after all, the uterus spends two-thirds of its life under the downward pulling force of gravity just as the rest of the body does. During pregnancy the uterus, together with its muscles, is stretched, and many gynecologists reckon that the average female can stand only three pregnancies before the uterus becomes strained. Additionally, most women spend far too much time on their feet, not only in jobs such as salesclerks but also in their homes at the kitchen sink!

The ligaments and muscles eventually give up under the strain, and the uterus flops a bit. It worsens, of course, and medical textbooks show lovely pictures of flopped wombs.

The set of muscles behind the uterus are in turn strained, and soon the back muscles are involved. Hence, the backache. As the uterus flops, it does so partly onto the bladder and tells the bladder falsely that it is full, so it keeps on wanting to empty itself even though very little urine is excreted.

Q. How do kidney stones start? What are they made of, and is it possible to live with them or do they have to be removed?

A. Kidney stones start as minute buildups of calcium, mixed with either phosphate or oxalate, upon the kidney tissues. Sometimes they remain in the kidneys indefinitely, causing little or no trouble, but if infection begins around them, trouble can ensue. The infection can further involve the kidneys and descend through the ureters into the bladder, causing cystitis with bleeding.

If the stone moves down in the expelled urine to either of the ureters, great efforts must be made to shift it. Usually the patient is hospitalized and given vast amounts of liquid to try to flush the stone out. The procedure takes a few days, and painkilling drugs are generally administered. If this fails, surgery is a possibility, because the obstructed flow of urine building up behind the stone becomes stale and infected from the poisonous substances in the urine.

Kidney stones can vary in size and number according to each patient, and only by X ray can the specialist come to the right diagnosis and treatment for his patient. If the stones keep recurring, the patient may eventually be seen by a nephrologist, who will investigate the patient's metabolism to find any discrepancies which might be causing the stones. He may prescribe a daily course of cranberry juice to counteract calcium stones.

Q. I have bladder cancer. I am told it is in its early stages, so there is hope. What treatments might I expect to encounter, and can I help toward their success?

A. Modern treatment for bladder cancer has improved so much that doctors are able to control the growth of the tumor and, in fact, arrest almost completely the spread of the first growth. This is achieved by diathermy coagulation—burning away of the tumor—and as it regrows, it is burned away again. A ten-minute operation every three or four months enables the patient to remain in good general health and to lead an active life. Again, speedy diagnosis is essential. High-protein diets and frequent feet-up sessions will keep the body strengthened and rested.

Q. Is it possible for a man to be a permanent carrier of _Trichomonas_ without necessarily reacting positively to tests?

A. First there are tests and tests! It is sometimes

possible for the common simple swabs to show negative results, particularly after a course of treatment has just ended. However, with persistent recurrence of symptoms in either the male or his sexual partner, it may become advisable for him to visit either a venereologist or a genitourinary specialist and embark on a more complex series of tests. These could involve the analysis of the male prostatic secretions from high in the prostate gland and also several urethral swabs. It is also necessary for the sexual partner to follow a course of treatment, since trichomoniasis is infectious.

Q. Is bad breath a recognized feature of urinary infection?

A. Bad breath is usually to be found in urinary disease only in terminal renal failure. You must look elsewhere for an answer to this problem.

Q. Why is dilatation of the urethra so often recommended by doctors, since it doesn't seem to work very effectively after a while?

A. A straight answer to this is that we don't really know. It certainly works temporarily in women who have interstitial cystitis. This is a rare condition of the bladder lining which, over two to four years, disintegrates and finally stops contracting altogether. Dilatation and drainage every four or six months helps a little, but the inevitable decision about removing the bladder has to be taken. For these women who have spent many months in misery and great pain, bladder removal affords great hope. Groups exist to give aid and encouragement to such sufferers, so seek out your nearest.

A kidney X ray may show a mechanical obstruction of some kind which would respond well to a dilatation of the bladder neck and urethra. Dilatation should be performed under a general anesthetic since the introduction of steel rods into the urethra is extremely painful. The idea is to stretch the urethra, during which process damage is done to the urethral tissue, causing scarring. Dilatations provide only temporary relief, so don't be disappointed when you realize that you are back to square one after three months. It is a fashionable operation performed far too frequently with little or no medical evidence to back up its suggested usefulness for women with recurrent cystitis.

Q. Could someone enlighten us about hard water, soft water, fluoride, chlorine, and so forth in the town's water supply?
A. There is no hard-and-fast evidence that any of the so-called trace elements in water have any bearing on urinary infection, but of course, in twenty years' time we may find that fluoride makes bacteria grow in peculiar places! With regard to other urinary problems there is some evidence that high calcium content predisposes toward urinary calculi. But as far as we know, there is no proof that trace elements contain infection-producing agents.

Q. I am keen to start another pregnancy, but under conditions of recurrent cystitis I am naturally hesitant. (A) Can it be passed to my future baby, and (B) can it prevent conception?
A. No is the answer to both these questions. Several members of a family may have urinary problems, but then this is also true of other illnesses. If investigation has been made and there is the possibility of the cystitis's being associated, say, with a

tropical disease, it may be well to have tests done on the child at a later date, but this is rather remote.

Cystitis certainly cannot prevent conception, but we feel it might be wise to point out that adding the extra work involved with small children to an already troubled woman could prove to be an added strain.

Q. Can you "imagine" cystitis? My doctor seems to think this is the reason.

A. In a minuscule number of cystitis cases there may be a psychological element. However, pain and blood loss are rarely psychological in origin, and until the doctor has absolute proof of his supposition, he would be wiser to search for physical rather than psychological causes. It would be unusual for a woman to invent clear symptoms and waste hours of her time and her doctor's and we think it silly to tell her to "go away and forget it." All relevant investigation is needed.

Q. Can urinary infection relate in any way to sore eyes and head pains?

A. Yes, UI can be associated with conjunctivitis. It calls for the fullest investigation by both your doctor and any specialists to whom he feels he should refer you. Action must be taken as quickly as possible.

10. Depression and Tension

There are two types of people who get depression: first, those with unstable minds for whom mental illness is as much a part of their health problem as physical illness. Second, people who become depressed because of circumstances in their lives.

During the 1960s it became the fashion for family doctors to tell a recurrent cystitis patient that he felt she was oversensitive. But as one woman explained:

> "The problem disappears when I am heavily enough tranquilized, but I do not wish to spend my life on tranquilizers. My doctor tells me to relax and forget it—quite impossible."

Thirty-five percent of women with recurrent cystitis are given tranquilizers in a futile and helpless act of medical surrender. When in the 1960s and early 1970s self-help was completely unknown to both doctors and patients, tranquilizers were administered to patients depressed by attacks of cysti-

tis. No hope of cessation of attacks was offered—
"You'll have to learn to live with it"—and the patient felt that life had nothing at all left to offer. With the cause of so many patients' attacks unknown, each of the failures knew that she was a failure. Severity and length of attacks, coupled with increasing frequency of attacks, would eventually prevent normal daily life.

To understand how one could become so fearful and frightened, some facts about attacks should be remembered.

1. Attacks of cystitis can occur at any hour of the day or night.

2. If sex is the cause, but the patient doesn't know why or what to do about it, intercourse becomes dreaded.

3. An attack can cause frightening blood loss.

4. The pain is unbelievably sharp. Take a kitchen knife, cut yourself, and douse the cut with vinegar for some idea of what that might feel like inside the urethra.

5. There is no lonelier place than a toilet and no lonelier woman than the one bearing down in involuntary urination.

6. Whence cometh my aid? It is 2:00 A.M. on Sunday. You live on a country hillside!

7. The family doctor will not visit you, and you must telephone him for a prescription or a few pills to tide you over.

8. The pills didn't help last time because here you are again.

9. Your husband is fed up to the teeth with your trouble.

10. Why me?

Such temporary distress has sent many women

to the nearest emergency ward, only to be turned away. This is not a matter of life and death, stitching or bandaging. "Your family doctor will deal with you."

The medical world is fed up with you, not to mention unhelpful, and your husband is frustrated and angry.

No comfort, no hope, no freedom from pain, only the knowledge that you are getting inexorably worse by the hour. No one will hold your hand and head as you sit screaming in your nightie in that toilet; no one understands your pain; no one understands how hopeless you feel; no one understands that you don't really see what there is left to live for.

Give it another five hours, and there is only a drop of urine at a time coming out of the urethral opening. On the toilet paper, when you look at it, is pure blood, no urine left to disguise its presence. There it is, bright red.

Because you can no longer stand, you wrap a towel around you like a diaper and stay in bed. Infection has now reached the kidneys, and you are very, very sleepy. Also very, very cold, so someone brings a hot-water bottle, maybe two, and you barely know what is going on around you.

Eventually antibiotics are administered, but you are well into the third morning before they start winning their battle with the infection. With such a violent attack it's bed for the week. There will be no Cousin Jimmy's wedding for you, no sex for you, no housework, no shopping, and no job for two weeks. There may be a heated argument and the minimum of words between you and your husband for a long while.

But even all that pales into insignificance beside

the uppermost worry in your mind: "I can't live with all this for much longer."

From here each woman takes a different path. Some travel around, trying as many specialists as possible; some do put up with it; some get divorced; some become psychiatric patients; some attempt suicide—one or two succeed; there are no statistics—and others? Others have heard of self-help.

A friend lends an old magazine article; another hears a talk on the radio; the bookshop orders *Cystitis: The Complete Self-help Guide* and now you try self-help.

The attitude of hopelessness is relieved. The subject is much more open in the media. The correct self-help will prevent attacks from starting.

Recurrent cystitis can cause depression; depression does not cause cystitis. Fortunately, this point is well and truly accepted by British doctors as a result of self-help work.

> "Family doctors may have appeared somewhat unsympathetic in the past—this is entirely because they too have felt foxed and helpless."—Consultant psychiatrist.

> "Having suffered acutely from urinary infections all my life since I was eleven, because of a variety of causes and unenlightened doctoring, I now find myself in my sixties having been unable to achieve very much in my life and regretting with all my heart the inheritance of such an unhealthy body. It has been and still is a drag on my otherwise-healthy mind."—Male.

> "Please don't fail me! I have suffered from this embarrassing handicap for years, and the hope which you hold out of being able to cope with attacks is like being born again."

"My husband, a most unreasonable bully, nearly raised the roof when he saw your leaflet on cystitis. He said I had been to specialists and having that 'morbid' literature coming into the house would make me imagine an attack even if I weren't having one!"

"Three years ago I had a complete nervous breakdown, and after a few days in a mental hospital my mother rescued me and nursed me herself. My husband had gone off to Norway with another woman because of my cystitis, which had been continuous since marriage. The only time it was better was during my pregnancy. I became very depressed from not only the attacks but also the drugs each time. This affects the disposition of the whole family, and I cannot take a job seriously, as I am unreliable."

The only hard-and-fast method of doing away with cystitis depression is not to get cystitis! The depression is a result of the recurrence and the drugs. Large, old-fashioned drug maintenance therapy is debilitating and depressing. It is such a slow and insidious feeling that the patient doesn't realize that the process is happening. For such a case it is best to know of this prospective trouble and question the large dose of drugs as it is being prescribed.

For depression during the attack itself, one can be more positive. The self-help management process keeps the patient busy and occupied for the worst part of the attack, and as it recedes, the notebook comes out. The notebook is for factual reporting of the forty-eight hours previous to the start, a time period which is particularly vital if the cause or causes of attacks are as yet unknown. If you know the cause, the notes are still useful in avoiding a recurrence of that same cause. Remember all you can about sex, alcohol, liquid, and so forth, and reread the self-help literature to refresh your memory. If you know what caused the current attack, then get on with doing something you enjoy. Have a chat with a friend on the phone, do some needlework, read a book, or if you are coping well, catch up with neglected work.

When you deal with an attack with the self-help management process, depression hardly ever occurs. There will be a certain amount of preliminary cursing if you are human, and that is good for you! Other than that, you can be assured of release from tears and helplessness each time.

In younger women, not being able to have sex plays a large part in recurrent cystitis depression. This is an additional misery which older women may not feel quite so strongly about. Being in love with your husband but unable to make love to him for fear of starting another attack of cystitis causes loss of confidence and lack of libido. Eventually you choose to reject his advances and to suppress your own sexual urge. Sometimes this automatically happens over a lengthy time span, and you may not even be aware of it; but other women make a definite decision to steer clear of sex—indeed, are often encouraged to do so by some gynecologists. But far from helping, abstinence increases the tensions in the patient's home. This advice has never been known to work, and if it's given to you, there is nothing to do but laugh at the person advising you, walk to the door, leave that room, and never bother to enter it again!

A human body and mind need certain minimum requirements to function:

Food
Water
Air
Sex.

Sex, when joyful, releases daily tensions and promotes happiness. Only when you have abstained for a long while is it possible to estimate the value of having intercourse. Life is in perspective with a regular sexual session, and although it is possible to go without it, you know when you miss it. Life loses the silver rim, the excitement of blue skies, and the spring in your shoes as you walk. Jobs become just jobs, not fulfillments; pain becomes pain, not something temporary; and worst of all, it is impossible to lift the black cloud when once you could.

Recognizing this depression as basically sexual if you are young can be halfway to counteracting it. The other half is for you and your partner to turn your sex life inside out for ideas on what is causing the cystitis after intercourse. Over a two-month period or less, treat sex almost clinically with stringent hygiene and careful movements. Doing it in slow motion for a while and experiencing improvements give heart and courage as the days go by, and if extra medical care is needed, pay for it. It would be money well spent. Sexual cystitis is almost 100 percent conquered by self-help. Take heart!

If severe depression as a result of intransigent urinary troubles does become a part of your life, don't go it alone. Use the help of a sympathetic psychotherapist or psychiatrist, and don't give up the physical battle. In these circumstances such experts are perhaps extra-kind and considerate, and it's like having a very understanding and interested friend. If you have horrible things happening to your bladder because doctors are doing their best to keep your condition from deteriorating, a psychotherapist working in full knowledge of such obnoxious but necessary actions will be most important. When life gets difficult, remember that one hundred years ago surgeons carved up penises and bladders without anesthetics!

When life becomes good for a while, whoop it up! You will have to whoop it up to the limit of your bladder restrictions, of course, but if one of your favorite foods is fresh shrimp, have a feast. If you cannot make it to a restaurant for a cheerful dressed-up-in-your-finery meal, have it at home instead. Send out for something you truly enjoy, or if you can *really* splurge, have a caterer come to your home. Get dressed up, put some flowers and candles on a nice white tablecloth, play some Mozart or Donna Summer and with a list of interesting current news topics to chat about, enjoy yourself.

Developing an indoor hobby which could eventually become lucrative is a stimulus in boring illnesses, and if you have decided to live rather than die, you have to find a counteraction to the depression. An indoor hobby is useful; so is becoming involved in any kind of charity or organization working on your illness. Fund raising in the tiniest ways brings a date to look forward to if you are housebound. There is a great satisfaction in collecting money to help combat or research your illness, and if it is combined with a social event, you get cheered up, too.

"Mind over matter" is a very old saying. It still holds true, so keep busy, in both work and pleasure.

"Thank you from the bottom of my heart for all the help. I have suffered with cystitis for ten years without much help or breaks in between the attacks. My nerves were wrecked, and without the new-found self-help I am sure I would have done something silly as I felt I didn't want to live."

11. Vacations

"A reader wrote of the horrors of being without a toilet abroad—I do so agree; my life seems to become bladder-oriented as soon as I set foot outside my country. My worst experience was in Tokyo, where the Japanese sign for 'ladies' is a sea gull with wings outstretched and a dot over its head!"

Well, thank goodness for that information! The object of a vacation is primarily to relax and withdraw from our normal routines. The possibilities can be tremendously varied; surely the choice has never been better. We can choose to do nothing but eat, sleep, swim, and have sex. We can go camping in a tent for two, drive across country, travel by bike. We can go on sea/plane cruises, island cruises, winter or summer cruises. There are hiking vacations, painting vacations, cookery vacations, visits to Greenland, jeeps across the Kalahari Desert. We can self-cater or be spoon-fed, walk or climb; go singly, in groups or just family; see ancient cities in the winter or the Andes in spring, the Taj Mahal by moonlight or a monastery at matins. If you want to do it, some travel agency will be delighted to help you!

Whatever you decide, if it is an experiment, you will be entering an unknown area of health, but for people suffering from bladder complaints, choice doesn't have to be all that limited. In fact, even a tour of the vineyards in Germany could be done with proper forethought.

Bladder patients are their own worst enemy on vacations. They think, "Aha! Vacation time. I'm going to enjoy myself and forget all my troubles."

Oh, no, you won't! Your bladder won't forget, and it will probably thoroughly object to your sudden relaxation of all the rules.

Thousands and thousands of vacation trips have been ruined by cystitis. Within three or four days some poor friends or relatives are finding you a local doctor, and you are holed up in a hotel bedroom, awaiting the arrival of antibiotics. Further travel, swimming, or sunbathing are out of the question, and not only do you look wistfully out of the bedroom window at your friends, but they are naturally concerned about you.

Bus tours can be vicious on the bladder, yet lots of bladder victims will take them! Bladders object to being sat on for hours on end. They are forced to endure pressure internally from building-up urine and pressure externally from the seat. The urethra gets squashed, and the old scars in it are strained. Even in a new luxurious bus carrying drinks and a toilet it takes courage to walk the length of that aisle several times a day. As for a full-blown attack under such circumstances, the natural agitation which accompanies attacks plus seating restrictions must be grim. If there is no toilet on board, having to request frequent stoppages is embarrassing to you and annoying to the other people around you. A train is a better bet. You can take exercise more frequently up and down the aisles, there is a good selection of soft drinks and hot beverages, there are toilets all over the place, and you arrive faster. For the small difference in price and the greater returns in comfort it must be folly for bladder patients to travel by bus whenever it can be avoided.

What about cars? In a car you are your own mistress, and the stress is greatly reduced particularly if you are traveling *à deux*. The same urethral and bladder pressures apply, though, and women who experience vibration disturbances appear to be less comfortable in smaller vehicles. A cushion helps, but if vibration is always a distress, even on half-hour trips, you will have to plan something else. Just because a car is out of the question, other forms of travel may not be. Canoeing might be just right for you. If you live in Great Britain, what about a canal barge? This is slow and effortless, and you can walk along the towpath with a horse if you've a mind. Or try a gypsy caravan, again horse-drawn, and sleeping in an inn each night. The hirer might be persuaded to bring it to your door!

Even with trains, you have options. Try an overnight sleeper to your destination, during which time your bladder will be quieter in a prone position. A five-day minicruise on a boat could be worth the experiment, and the following year try a longer one if the first trip was successful. Don't feel defeated; bend the rules a little, and try out any logical ideas.

Patients not quite in such predicaments with vibration reactions can manage the travel side all right but sometimes overreach themselves. A bicycling vacation is not a good idea! Picture the position of the urethra and vagina as you sit on a bicycle saddle. Your body is tilted forward, and the perineum is hard up against the leather seat beneath your pants. Frequently the external labia will separate, and that last cushion of defense will be removed. The urethra and vagina will be bruised and rubbed all day, every day for the duration of the vacation, and that alone is enough to start soreness and inflammation. But if, in addition, you swallow the local wine and have some sex, you will have to go to bed!

How about a hiking vacation, carrying all the necessary camping equipment? Only if you are on top of your troubles. If you are prepared to stick to the rules of prevention rigidly and are proficient in staving off those ominous twinges, try it. Have a vaginal checkup before you depart, since there's nothing worse than a drippy discharge with urethral involvement when you are far away from medical help. Sticking pessaries or cream up yourself on a bare mountainside can be unutterably miserable.

As for the physical effect of walking, all competent hikers have regulated stops every so often for a rest, and since hiking is usually done in country areas, there is no shortage of makeshift toilet facilities. If you are likely to sweat with all this physical effort, remember to replace the lost liquid and have several bland drinks.

Medical scientists have discovered that air travelers lose a lot of body liquid on long journeys. They think that this is a contributory factor in jet lag and one of the reasons why passengers sometimes feel lethargic for many days after the journey. A three- to four-hour air journey for the bladder patient should mean no alcohol during the voyage. Choose, instead, soda water or very milky coffee or any soft drinks to counteract this loss of body fluids. Change your sitting position from time to time to relieve seat pressure on the perineum, and have a few walks up and down the aisle.

Toilets other than your own should be treated very guardedly. Even if the bowl and seat look spotless, don't trust it. If paper seat covers are available, use them. Otherwise, tear off some tissue, and put three sheets on either side of the center. Sit on these with your legs wide apart so no other part of your bottom touches the bowl. In such manner, bowels or bladder may work properly, with neither catching any infection. It is possible to catch some infections from toilet seats, not syphilis or gonorrhea but possibly streptococci from someone else's boils or spots or maybe *E. coli* from little children's fingers. "Safety first in strange toilets" can never be amiss, and washing your hands after visiting the toilet means a good deal more after your hand has touched the flush mechanism. Try not to be caught without paper hankies in a pocket or purse. In strange toilets such a supply can be used in place of absent toilet paper and for the emergency washing routine after a bowel movement.

When you really seriously consider the sort of vacation that a woman prone to cystitis should take, it boils down to three kinds:

1. Your own toilet in your own van or trailer *or*—

2. Your own toilet *en suite* in a hotel *or*—

3. Your own toilet in a rented vacation apartment.

A vacation for bladder patients, if it is indeed to be a good one, means a tightening up of the rules and regulations. In response to the climate and to increased sexual activity all appropriate rules should be extended.

Hot climates prove immensely dangerous to cystitis sufferers unless they observe the rules of prevention. Since large amounts of body liquid are sweated out under the sun, a greater intake of water is absolutely vital. A normal vacation drinking routine for nonsufferers includes strong coffee at breakfast, prelunch alcohol, wine with lunch, followed by more black coffee. The afternoon often includes a soft drink, tea or more coffee, then cocktails, more wine, and more coffee. The grand total is probably one and a half pints of strong coffee, one to one and one-quarter bottles of wine, three to four cocktails, and one soft drink. That is what a cystitis sufferer could find herself drinking in an attempt to enjoy herself, forget her troubles, and appear normal.

If the unenlightened cystitis-prone woman does this and adds spicy foods, numerous sexual episodes, plus a morning and afternoon swim, she will be twinging within thirty-six hours. If you have had countless vacations ruined by cystitis, here are your vacation drinking rules:

Breakfast
    1 large glass of bottled water upon arising
    1 large breakfast cup or more of milky coffee or tea

Midmorning
    2 tumblers of any soft low-calorie canned drink (*not* a concentrated juice)

Lunch

1 small sherry or 1 small vermouth, et cetera, with soda, lemonade, tonic

1 glass of bottled water

1 glass of a light wine, red or white, but light

1 large cup of milky coffee

Midafternoon

1 or more canned soft drinks or 1 large weak tea or more bottled water

Dinner

1 glass of bottled water, followed by:

Aperitif as for lunch

2 glasses of a light wine

Some bottled water

Small black coffee.

This time, totals are roughly as follows:

Pure bottled water, 4 to 5 pints

Just over ½ bottle of wine

¾ pint of optional coffee and tea

2 pints of soft drinks.

Liquid intake overall is around seven to eight pints. This is a comfortable amount to drink in one day and allows for sweating as well as for reasonable urine flow. Increase the intake if necessary, but under no circumstances consume less. The alcoholic drinks are nicely sandwiched and should cause no trouble. Very important in the early morning is bottled water because it will give the kidneys a bland start and flush out any collecting traces of uric acid.

If you have intercourse at night in hot climates, make up for the excitement and lost liquid sweated or passed by drinking more of that bottled water. Should you be in a country that doesn't have a supply of bottled mineral water, substitute tonic or soda. Don't risk the local tap water unless there are boiling facilities in your bedroom.

If you find yourself somewhere in Africa or other continents where the tap water looks murky, shower each night, but afterward rinse the urethra, vagina, and anus with any kind of noncarbonated bottled water—in other words, the same as what you are drinking.

Swimming pool water and seawater are sources of trouble. In a pool there are other people's germs and chlorine. Chlorine and other people's germs flow in and out of your vagina. Germs are germs, but chlorine is highly irritating to mucous membranes. Do you sneeze after swimming or sound blocked up when you speak? That is the effect of chlorine, and it is probably upsetting the vagina just as much as it upsets your nasal passages. A daily or twice-daily dip for a few days will find inflammation in the vagina plus the added hazard that chlorine is an antibacterial chemical. As such, all bacteria die, and the way is open, as with antibiotics, for disturbance of your skin's defense system. Fungus infections like moniliasis and candidiasis will invade the defenseless skin and grow quickly, putting a stop to intercourse and giving you itchy, disturbed nights.

Seawater can contain effluent chemicals or sewage, sand, and salt particles. Every time you open your legs to kick underwater some of these products will enter your vagina. Sand will get trapped in the gussets of your swimwear and will chafe the skin; salt will sting; and the rest? It doesn't bear thinking about!

The answer is simple. No, it isn't to give up such enjoyment but to try to negate its harmful effects. Go straight afterward for a shower or take with you into the toilet some water in a bottle. Sit down on the arranged toilet tissues, and pour the bottled water over your perineum. Part the labia with your free hand, and also penetrate the vagina, allowing as much water as possible in to wash out any hazards. Change the swimwear for one previously rinsed free of salt, sand, and chlorine and ready for wearing. The dry swimwear will also prevent an excitement of the kidneys, caused by chilling.

This way you can swim often, but don't forget to rinse the perineum really well and take several swimming costumes.

If your vacation hideaway is so secluded that you can indulge in sex at any time, don't do it immediately on leaving the pool—rinse off first, both of you!

Sun, sea, sex, and champagne are the main ingredients for vacation and honeymoon cystitis. Have them all, certainly, but be helpful to your bladder as well.

Clothing should be appropriate to the weather. If hot days give place to cool nights, take a wrap and at least one dress with long sleeves. If your evening wear is long, go without pants. No one will see, and your tiring perineum can have a good airing. Air is very good for it, so give it three or four hours' airing each evening. If you are touring in a van or camping, keep warm but not by enveloping your perineum in nylon or tight jeans. A divided woolen skirt and a pair of warm cotton pants will do nicely. Long boots and long woolen socks will keep the legs and the tops of the legs very warm and pretty.

Always take the cystitis management kit with you when you go away. If you get blasé and think your prevention is so good that you will defy the gods and leave it behind, there is no doubt that the gods will laugh and promptly descend! The most tightly packed suitcase has room for the kit. It should also have a hot-water bottle and plenty of painkillers. Water-purifying tablets could be useful, and so, unhappily, might some antibiotics. Don't take them unless the self-help management process completely fails and you are sure you have a really virulent infection.

Should a vaginal discharge start, go for a swab somewhere, anywhere, and don't start creaming yourself haphazardly; you will probably make the condition worse. Stop intercourse, and leave the prescribed pessaries to work in peace. Don't bathe, don't swim, and keep a close watch for any bladder involvement. If this happens, start drinking a half pint of water every hour to keep the bladder clean, but if you have started the vaginal therapy, it may not be necessary to start the full-scale self-help management process.

If you bring on an attack with too much sex and careless alcoholic intake—very common on vacations—take a teaspoonful of bicarbonate immediately, and push as much water down your throat as you can manage. Rest up, and stop sightseeing for twelve hours. Take off restrictive clothing, don't sunbathe either, and swab your perineum with cool, soothing water. After twelve hours you may still feel the physical effects of your folly, but keep a maintenance water intake of about a pint every two hours,

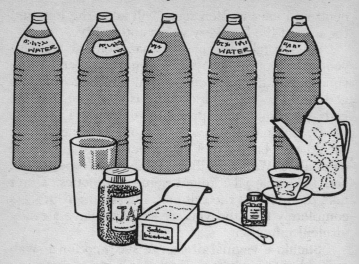

and forgo sex until all twinges and soreness disappear—they will. Don't eat antibiotics just because you have had too much sex and alcohol—there are no germs, only excess acidity and sore, bruised perineal skin.

With sex high on the vacation hazard list, remember to take a new, full tube of KY jelly. You've won a real battle if you have three sexual episodes a day and an empty KY jelly tube after two weeks. Well done!

Do enjoy your vacation. The encouragement of a cystitis-free vacation is joy unbounded, a pinnacle of success after years of disappointments. What you have achieved is power over your body's weak point, and your pride in yourself is well deserved.

12. Discharges

Any discharge from the vagina, whether small or embarrassingly copious, should be put under a microscope as soon as possible. It is not possible to give an accurate diagnosis any other way. Lay medico/social workers can certainly be trained to "read" a microscope slide and identify common bacteria; indeed, that is how laboratory analysts first start. Inserting a speculum into the vagina can also be taught to a lay person. In fact, if you are in an *isolated* situation but know of a laboratory capable of analyzing vaginal swabs, go there. Request a sterile swab kit, and retire to a ladies' room, locking the door behind you. Lie on the floor on your back, and cleanse the vaginal orifice with a piece of wet cotton; remove the swab stick from its container; then draw up both legs, and gently push the stick up the vagina as far as it will go. Move it around a bit, and then gently remove it. Replace the stick in the container, and put the lid on. Give it as quickly as possible to the analyst, and wait for the initial diagnosis.

He or she will be able to give an accurate first reaction but will subsequently put the mucus in a blood agar for further analysis.

If your current discharge has occurred in your home area, there is a choice of investigative approaches. In the past five or six years American family doctors have been gaining ground which was previously held by specialty doctors. Using the family doctor for all the family ills has been out of favor probably because specialists, able to charge higher fees, were able to give better services. So patients became used to using such consultants—that is to say, those working in only one field of medicine. With vastly increased specialty bills, patients have begun to patronize the cheaper family doctor. He, in turn, has started to receive proportionately higher fees and with increasing knowledge and more sophisticated equipment can now encroach on territories of care formerly offered only by consultants.

In health centers where more than one family doctor practices there are obviously more services to offer. Many doctors in America at family level will happily take vaginal swabs and view the vaginal mucus under their own microscopes. For the legal safety of both parties a chaperone, usually an involved female member of the practice staff, will be present. The chaperone's job is to be basically handy with a light, instrument passing, or the patient's sweaty palm!

Any family doctor caring enough to provide this service will have the basic knowledge of bacteria to read the microscope results. For a vaginal discharge he will easily recognize yeast infections, pus cells, epithelial cells (the normal molting that happens with vaginal skin), *Trichomonas,* nonspecific infections, and maybe some others.

Any doctor who fails to examine a vaginal discharge or take swabs of it for microscopic examination isn't worth your money. There are different discharges for every month of the year, requiring quite different medication but often with very similar symptoms like irritation and redness. Discharges must be examined and microscoped at all times.

If you are prone to frequent vaginitis or perineal troubles and have good private health insurance, you may prefer to use a gynecologist every time. Don't be frightened of having second opinions, though, if over a long period of time your "favorite" has not been as helpful as you'd like. Any gynecologist who doesn't logically explain what he or she thinks is wrong with you, who suggests operations rather too quickly, who rejects your ideas with pomposity, who reaches a shade too quickly for the prescription pad, or who in any way gives you cause for uneasiness is not worth your unease. If you're paying good money, you expect good treatment in both the medical and the human sense.

Planned parenthood groups are basically for that, remember. Discharges will doubtless be dealt with, but PP is a place to go for abortion, contraception, and counseling.

When you suspect that you have vaginal trouble, you may choose to find the nearest venereology department. Perhaps it is called a discharge clinic, VD clinic, or special clinic. Telephone your nearest big hospital for information on clinical availability. Do whatever is specified, and just turn up at the agreed time. You need take nothing with you.

Such departments are improving tremendously

in their style. Many have music, carpets, and lounge chairs; most have pleasant waiting rooms and magazines. Even if your nearest clinic has no such delights but is bare and antiseptic, use it. The microscope is what you want. This is the only way anyone can know what is truly wrong with you.

A white-coated consultant will chat with you in a very sensitive manner. He is not going to pressure you about sexual subjects but is interested only in what your symptoms are and how they are affecting the vagina. After a few minutes a nurse will show you where to go to remove your underwear. If you wear crotchless panty hose, as you should, only your pants have to be removed.

The stirrup couch is hardly elegant, but then it wasn't designed to embellish the room. It was designed to enable the consultant to do his job properly; hence, the couch is quite high, with a couple of steps up. In order that the consultant can have the best view possible of your perineum, he must sit quite close, so the couch is just long enough to support the trunk of the body, not the legs. Each leg goes onto its own leg rest, and the consultant sits on his little black stool between them. A nurse adjusts the lights, passes the swab sticks, antisepticizes the couch paper, sterilizes the speculums, labels the specimens, and smiles at the patient!

Blood tests are usually done on one sample taken from a good vein, and if, for instance, you have recently returned from Africa, the consultant can order parasite tests on that sample as well. If anemia is suspected, a count is also taken off the same sample. This blood is analyzed in the hematology (blood) unit, and the results will not be available for two to three days.

During the physical examination there will be no pain. If you are already in pain and discomfort, don't hesitate to retell the consultant as he is about to look inside. When you can see and feel that he is being really careful, your next job is to relax, both your abdomen and your vagina. Breathe deeply a couple of times, and then flutter your breath if you begin to tighten up. Think, if you can, of how your vagina accepts a penis, and that will help. Slacken the walls, and think wide.

The consultant will tell you when he is about to slide in the speculum. This has rounded edges and cannot even tweak your skin. Unless this is inserted to prop open the walls of the vagina, nothing can be seen despite the light on the end of it, which is beautifully warm and quite comforting.

At first the consultant will just look and "discover" the vagina since no two are identical. He will be looking for blood, operation scars, polyps, warts, or anything strange, as well as for your discharge. The nurse will then hand him the swab stick, and the consultant will reassure you; but it is unnecessary. All he will do is gather some of the discharge on the cotton at the end of the stick and remove it.

The nurse will smear some discharge on a slide and then put the stick with the remaining mucus back in its container to be sent to the bacteriology department. The slide with the fresh mucus is carried immediately to the microscope and read.

The consultant should take three of these swabs: a high one from the cervix showing if the discharge is leaving the uterus, a middle vaginal swab giving an accurate review of its content, and a perineal/urethral swab taken just at the urethral opening. Now the microscope is able to give an accurate assessment of the state of health of your entire lower reproductive system.

At this stage try to direct the consultant's attention to any sore areas as his fingers move if you have trouble apart from any discharge. (If you have no discharge but have gone for examination because something else is wrong, the total examination as described will still be carried out.)

If bowels are in the slightest bit involved, the consultant will insert two fingers into the rectum and feel around to determine if anything is out of place or lumpy where it shouldn't be lumpy! This doesn't hurt either, and if you feel embarrassed, remember the rubber gloves which the consultant wears are disposable and unemotional.

At some stage, probably before the examination, you may be given a small bowl to pass some urine into. If you are having urinary symptoms in response to the discharge, most certainly a urine sample will be taken and given the same treatment as the mucus—some will be placed instantly under the microscope, and the rest will go to the bacteriology unit for two and one half days.

This is the way that all discharges should be approached. All need medical help, and the quicker the patient seeks that help, the sooner the trouble will disappear.

If you get an attack or have a continual fight with discharges, there are some important points to remember which will help ensure a quicker recovery:

1. Getting into a hot bath will make matters worse. Any inflammation is made worse by heat, so keep out of a bath. This is particularly important if you have a yeast infection. The fungus grows not

only in heat but also in moisture, and that is what a bath is—hot and wet. During discharges have only a quick shower or stand-up washes, and use cotton to cleanse the perineum. If you suffer from continual or difficult yeast infection, don't get in the bath for two months.

2. Change your underwear twice daily and boil it, or wear a small, thin pad—not one that has a layer of plastic underneath which will prevent air from helping heal the inflamed areas.

3. Walking a lot will only spread the discharge, and wet skin rubbing will increase the irritation.

4. Sitting in the same position for hours at a time will also exacerbate the inflammation.

5. Step up your liquid intake in order to abort any tendency by the discharge to infect the urethra. Keep the bladder gently flushing through.

6. Don't have intercourse until the treatment is finished, and when you start again, use the condom for a while.

7. Make sure your sexual partner is checked out as well in the venereology unit. If he is infected but not necessarily showing symptoms, the first time you have intercourse again will see you reinfected.

The majority of discharges are self-induced; that means they are preventable.

Trichomoniasis

This is a highly inflammatory and runny discharge. Patients experiencing their first attack often think they are passing urine against their will. Batches of liquid suddenly rush out of somewhere and are highly embarrassing. The liquid is clear but will dry out on underwear just like urine in a kind of brownish stain. This bacteria dies on contact with air; this means a microscope on site at diagnosis is the only way to isolate it. Trichomoniasis is contagious between sexual partners and thus is termed sexually transmittable. Apart from catching it from someone, there is one other way in which this infection arises. Mostly this happens because of poor hygiene and toilet bowl splashing. German women avoid this splashing by putting tissue paper in the toilet before they pass a stool. Women correctly employing the washing routines should never get trichomoniasis. If you do, seek immediate medical help, and drag your partner along as well. Both will be given a ten-day course of Flagyl tablets to take simultaneously even if symptoms do not appear present in the male. The usual rule—no sex until clearance swabs are taken—applies, and afterward both of you should revitalize perhaps tiring hygiene rules. Hygiene rules can never be entirely relaxed except at your peril.

Herpes

Genital herpes is on the increase. The worst part of having herpes is that once in your system, it never goes away. It is a virus caught by contact with a carrier, either by kissing someone with a cold sore or by having intercourse with someone who has remaining inflammation after a sore. Males with consistent tendencies toward herpes have been found to have attacks coinciding with vaginal kissing or generalized oral/genital contact. The natural vaginal lubricants contain some unknown factor (maybe the acidity) which triggers off the virus. Likewise, it is thought, the saliva and nasal mucosa may carry or trigger off the virus.

Herpes is scabrous. It looks like a bad knee graze with a layer of scab and in severe cases can cover an entire lip and nostrils, lasting for about three weeks. Genital herpes in its most severe form can be triggered off by perfectly ordinary missionary intercourse, the sexual liquids being the stumbling block. Such severity happening regularly will bring sex life to a complete halt perhaps for many years. Other people will be lucky and get it only when there has been oral/genital contact. Use of a condom is helpful.

It is felt in venereology circles that the increase of pornography and sexually "enlightened" articles has provoked many more people into using oral/genital sex. To their cost, an increasing number of experimenters find themselves actually having less sex as a result, because of sexual illness.

Cervical Erosion

This is dealt with in the chapter headed "Questioners' Forum." If you have repeated vaginitis from the erosion, a gynecologist should perform a cauterization, because the condition will only worsen. If you have to wait for this operation, the condom reduces the possibility of infecting your sexual partner.

Vaginal Warts

These are simply an overgrowth of cells which becomes hardened. During intercourse they are rubbed or damaged and probably bleed a little. Some pain may also be expected. Cauterization under a general anesthetic will remove these small protuberances, and a break from sex for three or four weeks until the skin is firm and healed is recommended.

In recent years a surgical instruments firm has perfected a useful and painfree method of removing polyps and warts without cautery or the need for a general anesthetic. Even a local anesthetic is unnecessary since the technique is one of using cold as opposed to burning. Cryosurgery is performed on an ordinary couch by the gynecologist using a cryoprobe. The entire process lasts ninety seconds without any discomfort at all, and the patient feels only a slight cervical ache for the rest of the day. With the old cauterization process there is bleeding for a few days and a messy discharge as well as time taken for hospitalization, anesthetic recovery, and damaged tissues to heal.

Vaginal and cervical polyps have a similar effect to that of warts, except that they are spongy rather than hard. Pain is not usually experienced, but they will bleed a little during intercourse. Cauterization or cryosurgery is again indicated, because leaving an open bleeding patch in the vagina can lead to later infections.

Noninfective Leukorrhea

This condition manifests itself in a white discharge often mistaken for candidiasis. The microscope report will not, however, reveal the presence of any trouble. In the vagina, as in the entire body, are cells which break free of the skin layers when their lives end. Normally they pass down and out in normal daily secretions, but sometimes too many break free and form a kind of discharge. The disintegrating cells chafe at tender skin and can involve the urethra just as other foreign bodies will.

Infection can begin since bacteria always thrive in stale secretions, so hygiene becomes extra-important. Sometimes these cells come away for no real reason other than just a molting period, the way hair does in the autumn. Sometimes noninfective leukorrhea is an early signal of pregnancy and is obviously induced by extra hormone activity preparing the uterus to care for the newly fertilized egg. Hygiene is the only way to ease the irritation. This again is best done by pouring cool water from a bottle onto the perineum in preference to a hot inflammatory bath.

Commencing the Pill has a similar effect and a similar hormonal explanation. The family planning doctor may advise a simple warm-water douche if there is a high prolific discharge, but frequent cotton-ball cleansing is sufficient to reduce this irritation to a controllable level.

Mixed Infections

These are exactly what their name implies: a mixture of all sorts of vaginal oddments with a few pus cells shown under the microscope. Pus indicates an infection, and doubtless the patient will have a discharge with it. Sometimes with good hygiene

mixed infections cause no soreness, irritation, or urethral involvement but are simply nuisances. Others
cause more trouble, but both should be dealt with
quickly in the venereology unit since they will not
go away without medical intervention. Stricter hygiene is helpful, and a source of infection can be the
"bottom" facecloth if it is not boiled or changed daily. Sex should be forgone until swabs give you clearance from symptoms, and it is again sensible for
your partner to have a checkup, particularly if he is
uncircumcised.

Worms

Rectal worms (the commonest sort is the
threadworm, which looks like thin white hairs about
one-half inch long) are often found in homes with
small children. This is because the children play
with dirt, sand, grass, and so forth, and get the minute worm eggs under their nails as well as on their
hands. One child with worms in a family can infect
the entire household. A child's anus should be examined at night for signs of scratching or for the actual
worms, since they emerge from the anus at night.
Unexplained, unremitting vaginal irritations or infections can be caused by anal worms. Deworming
pills will end the trouble. These vaginal problems
can be caused by worms in a small girl as well as in
her mother.

Yeast Infections

Yeast infections (also known as moniliasis, candidiasis, or vaginal thrush) are extremely common. In

fact, medical personnel reckon their incidence is now epidemic. The problem was almost unknown in great-grandmama's day. She had none of our modern precipitating factors but lived subconsciously, treating her body correctly.

To understand this, we must know what yeast is and how it breeds. It is a fungus infection which invades unhealthy or debilitated mucus membranes. The mouth, intestines, bowels, and genital organs are the most common areas in which this ailment thrives. Babies get yeast infections of the mouth; small children get them; so do adult men and women.

Yeast breeds in warmth, moisture, and sugar; that explains their favorite breeding grounds in the body. The infection is creamy in color and highly irritant, stains underwear, and can, if not understood, return again and again to plague the sufferer. This woman's history is, unfortunately, not uncommon:

> "I have suffered with this for the last five years very severely. I have scratched myself so much that I have made myself bleed."

Many cystitis sufferers experience this fungal invasion in addition to their bladder troubles, and this kind is almost entirely caused by their doctor. Cystitis, unless the patient employs self-help, is treated by antibiotics, and with large repeated antibiotic therapy the body becomes very debilitated, leaving the way open for fungus infiltration. When such infiltration occurs, its effects are inevitably felt in the urethra. But the patient and doctor believe that a recurrence of cystitis is happening, and even more antibiotics are administered, exacerbating recurring yeast infections.

Men, women, or children who are prone to these problems should always be given anti-fungal tablets, like Mycostatin or Lactinex, concurrently with a prescription for antibiotics. Such patients can try to do without antibiotics unless they really are essential. Yeast victims seem to do better on short, sharp antibiotic therapy rather than long-drawn-out doses. The lingering effects of a course of antibiotics can continue for four to six weeks, longer sometimes, after the course has ended, so be patient and helpful to yourself.

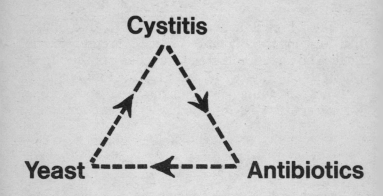

If you are on the pictured triangle, antibiotics are not the answer. Treat the attack of yeast as ordered by the doctor, but increase the liquid intake for as long as necessary to keep it from climbing the adjoining urethra. This could involve having a long drink every hour of your waking day until the condition is cleared and the aftereffects of antibiotics are worn off. This is the only way to get off that vicious chain reaction. Some women don't get off it for years, and the resulting marital/sexual damage can be very extensive.

Great-grandmama never experienced yeast side effects from antibiotics—they didn't exist. If she had a bad chest infection, she went to bed, kept warm, inhaled friar's balsam, took some painkiller, and sweated it out—or died.

Antibiotics in either sex or at any age, taken for any body illness at all, are still capable of causing a yeast infection. If a man has this resulting from a course of antibiotics for, say, an eye infection, he can still pass it on to his sex partner.

It is sexually transmittable.

Persistent infections in women can be attributable to hormone disturbance. Often, a patient under questioning remarks that it always seems to begin or worsen just before a period. Hormone changes at that time affect the skin in the vagina, slightly altering its acid/alkaline balance. Yeast finds a foothold and grows quickly. The same thing happens when some women begin using the Pill. Noninfective leukorrhea and yeast become muddled up, and only a microscope will reveal the true condition.

Patients could try using a weak vinegar-and-water douche at this time to counteract the acid/alkaline changes.

Great-grandmama did not have the Pill. To counteract possible irritation before a period, she left off her underwear.

Diabetes is the only illness which has yeast as a predestined side effect that is unpreventable. Only if the diabetes is carefully controlled by a daily insulin injection to reduce the sugar content in the blood can the yeast side effect be controlled. There is a condition known as prediabetes, in which bloodstream sugar is measured in varying excessive stages before the condition finally becomes true diabetes.

Prediabetes is worsened by daily sugar intake, such as two teaspoonfuls of sugar for every cup of tea or coffee and compulsive dessert eating. Many of these patients reveal a high weekly cookie intake.

Prediabetes is a fairly common cause of yeast in children because of their habits of eating sweets. Cut this down or even out. Cookies are unnecessary to good health and indeed seem to have only harmful effects. Men in the prediabetes stage who consume a lot of alcohol are also increasing their susceptibility to yeast. In men, it shows up mostly on the tongue or as stomach wind, so alcoholic effects can be demonstrated by cutting or reducing alcohol for a month or more and noting the difference.

The current epidemic of yeast infections really stems from another source. In the 1960s skirt hem lengths rose. Hosiery manufacturers seized upon the opportunity to design stockings that went higher up the leg in order to make women decently presentable.

Panty hose were introduced and over this last decade have entirely cornered the hosiery market. Nylon materials, including those from which panty hose are made, are impervious to air. Air is this planet's main drying agent. We dry our hair in hot air, hang our clothes in the garden to dry, and use air in countless ways for drying purposes.

Normal circulating air doesn't have the kind of force necessary to penetrate the close-knit weave of nylon panty hose. Without that supply of air a female perineum retains moisture which the skin areas of the crotch sweat out. All skin secretes liquid from its pores, and the compact area of thighs and perineum creates more perspiration than others. If air doesn't dry it off, it remains wet. Nylon makes for a sweaty crotch.

Skin is warm, and the perineum is normally very warm. Combining this warmth with the lack of sweat absorption creates the two conditions necessary for yeast to thrive.

Thus, the advent of panty hose has been instrumental in overheating and underdrying women's perinea. With a tight panty girdle over the nylon panty hose and over those pretty, but ruinous, nylon bikini pants, young and old women are encased in three highly unhealthy layers of nylon.

When miniskirts at last became unfashionable, the next and final stage in the breakdown of female sexual health arrived: jeans or trousers. These provided a fourth barrier to natural healing and cooling air. It is significant that:

1. Women are now more sexually unhealthy than ever in their history.

2. Women in hot countries do not wear panty hose or trousers and have no noted incidence of yeast infections.

Jeans and trousers came in with so-called women's liberation in an attempt initially to look equal to men. This idea gradually infiltrated all age-groups as the eroticism of tight jeans took on a visual aspect. Men encouraged girls to wear such exciting fashion, and older women anxious to appear "with it" also began to buy trousers.

This liberation process effectively attained the opposite. A smelly, oozy vagina irritating its owner to screaming pitch is no invitation to sexual adventures. Apart from being simply a fourth air barrier, tight jeans rub together when one walks. The rubbing causes friction, and friction causes heat, which is added to the already-trapped perineal heat. The heat causes even more sweating, so yeast, in the

1970s, became a commonplace sexually transmittable disease.

Women, to their cost, are learning this. Pressure has filtered through to lingerie and hosiery manufacturers requesting insertion of cotton gussets into panty hose and panties. Unfortunately they have failed to understand that with the keeping of an outer layer of nylon on the main body of the garment the cotton gusset is completely defeated.

Panties should be entirely made of cotton, and the designs updated. For winter, women should wear a thicker cotton, prettily pantalooned with ribbons and bows. Panty hose should be entirely crotchless. Panty girdles should have removable cotton gussets without a nylon overlay.

Jeans should die out of fashion—men have made enormous fortunes at the expense of women's health. Trousers should be low-crotched and made of lightweight wool tweeds; they should be worn only with cotton panties and knee-highs.

Long skirts like those of great-grandmama, perhaps more tailored, are the answer to yeast. At home, panties become superfluous, since long petticoats and overskirts prevent prying eyes.

Just one afternoon of nylon underwear or jeans will be enough to trigger off a yeast attack in susceptible women. Trying to ward it off by introducing yoghurt is a liberationist myth. The normal, healthy vagina is acidic but shows varying degrees of alkalinity toward menstruation. A strong swing toward alkalinity in some women is usually the reason why they get recurrent yeast attacks specifically before a period.

If you feel sure that this problem is undoubtedly recurring each month, you might try adding one teaspoonful of malt vinegar each night to your bottle of lukewarm water which is poured over the perineum for hygiene. It is important still to remember that washing is basically to be avoided during an attack of the fungus. So wash after passing a stool and as described above last thing at night.

Hot baths will not only make yeast inflammation twice as bad during the outbreak itself but also *cause* attacks in many women. Great-grandmama had a bath once a week in a tin tub before the kitchen fire. It cooled pretty fast, and she didn't soak in it. For the rest of the week she had stand-up washes, using her specially boiled rags, and she was much healthier than we are.

Regular swimming sessions in chlorinated pools create conditions under which yeast thrives, and such daily dips may have to stop if showering afterward will not keep this fungus away. Lots of women play sports in panty hose, rather than show pale, insipid legs. Panty hose are wicked in normal routines, but all boundaries of perineal heat and sweat are broken when they are worn in sports.

Anything in your life that triggers yeast infections should be stopped. For instance, many office girls sit all day on chairs with nylon or nylon mixture coverings. No air gets to their perinea, and the same predisposition exists. All the ideas in this chapter should provoke you into knowledge and prevention. Yeast infection is entirely preventable. It is never incurable except in diabetes, and then it is possible with stringent preventive rules, as outlined, to reduce it to a tolerable level.

Treatment for yeast by doctors varies. There are many pessaries and tablets most effective when used together orally and locally. If recurrence has taken place over a great many years, you may have a patch of easily aroused irritation in the pubic hair. When this itches, block it immediately with a smear of any hydrocortisone cream. Never use creams inside the labia because they will be self-irritating, but for pouncing on external labial irritation they are efficient. If you allow a labial or pubic itch to extend, it will not take long to reach the vagina. Pubic irritation will be helped greatly if you cut the pubic hair to a half inch or one inch in length. The difference in comfort can be gauged when the hair grows to irritation pitch once more. Shaving this hair or using a depilatory will set up irritation and soreness without any discharge present.

Yeast is a curse on female sexuality. We have to learn about it and accept that not all modern inventions, whether drugs or materials, are exactly kind to our bodies. But with thought it is possible to keep the benefits and eradicate the troubles.

13. Chemical Contamination

Since so much cystitis and vaginitis are self-induced, it becomes obvious that removal of the self-inflicted cause is prevention in its truest form. The major rules of increasing liquid intake to prevent external infections from ascending inside the urethra and bladder apply whatever the inflammation. Modern medicine can treat the inflammation, but it cannot remove many of the causes.

You can.

Here is a quote from a letter sent in response to a newspaper item on vaginal deodorants:

> "I wash every day, but one hot day I bought a deodorant spray because I used to wear a panty girdle and trousers. After using the spray for two or three mornings, I began to have pain in passing urine. I thought I had a chill and stopped using the spray. The condition cleared in a week. The spray remained forgotten until two weeks ago, when I found it and began to use it again. For three mornings I used it very lavishly in the rectal area as well

as the vaginal area because the scent was pleasant.
Once again I had great pain in passing urine and frequency. I felt very ill for the rest of the week but by
chance read last Sunday's item about the dangers of
vaginal sprays. Today I feel quite better again but
am scared to think of what is being done to us all and
how little aware of it we are."

Only this sort of personal experience seems to
stop women from being gullible and buying man-
made sexual money spinners. Manufacturers of toiletries don't care about the effects of their products
on women's health. They are a bit more careful over
babies' products, but it is only government consumer safety regulations that put any rein at all on the
ingredients of toiletries.

More and more women are becoming allergic to
facial cosmetics as "newer and better" chemical substances are researched, ever with an eye to costs.
Pure ingredients do not exist cheaply anymore; neither would there be enough to meet demand, so
substitutes are always being used experimentally.
Years ago, when women made soap from tallow ex-
tracted from boiling sheep or goat fat, it was pure
but didn't smell very good. They added herbs from
their vegetable patch or flower petals from the
heavily perfumed varieties like lavender. The soap
was still pure and remained so for centuries.

In the late nineteenth century, when the Indus-
trial Revolution was in full swing, men's minds
turned to factory manufacture of all manner of
goods on a large scale.

Any women's market was known to be reward-
ing, and so began the highly successful exploitation
of mass toiletry products. Pure homemade soap, for
instance, was removed to the men's domain and

manufactured en masse for a busy working nation. Carbolic soap was first used for scrubbing kitchen work surfaces and butcher shops, then used in Europe in hospitals for women lying in. It was proved to be a key factor in preventing puerperal fever, childbirth fever, when mothers who caught it usually died. Surgeons began to use it in general for hygienic scrubbing up before operations, and the high postoperative infection rates began to decrease.

A bright manufacturer somewhere decided that what was good in hospitals must be good in the home, and for many years carbolic soap was a general-purpose household soap. It left the hands and face like sandpaper, so in response to pressures, manufacturers began to add softeners and perfumes and creams until pure soap was no longer obtainable.

Coloring agents, perfumes, and paddings have now reached saturation point, and we women buy soap for its perfume and color, not for its purity. Antiseptic soaps have always had a strong market position, because housewives are accountable for family health and hygiene, and they think that anything antiseptic must clear away bacteria and be a health-giving aid in the reduction of infection.

Women with cystitis or vaginitis, in despair at trying to do away with the infections from which they suffer, go out and buy strong antiseptic soaps— to their cost, because soon they add inflammatory contamination to their existing troubles and mask the true source of their cystitis. Mothers will mistakenly use the same soap on little girls' sore bottoms, and the resultant suffering is pitiable.

In recent years deodorizing soaps which claim to eliminate personal odors and maintain daylong freshness have arrived on the market. The makers are adding more and suspect chemicals which produce skin reactions, and women still have not taken a stand. They buy without question any toiletry so long as it is prettily packaged, smells beautiful, and goes with the bathroom color scheme. The money being made out of our stupidity and gullibility runs into millions of dollars a year. There are no stringent restrictions on these products, since they are not classed as drugs and therefore are regarded as not dangerous. New toiletries are given only hasty and biased checks, if at all, by the manufacturers, who do not test them over a lengthy period.

On the drugstore counters are potentially harmful toiletries ready to be taken home in exchange for a few pieces of silver. Not that a customer is necessarily safe if she chooses a product of many years' standing. A new managing director or research chemist in that product's company has only to decide to update the product, and it becomes as hazardous as something brand-new.

When one chooses soaps, the safest way is to go for the one that claims to have no additives, no perfumes, no colorants, no antiseptics. There are always a couple like this in every drugstore, but when you've bought it, don't immediately race home and soap the perineum all over. Soap is quite unnecessary and harmful when used over the vagina and urethra. It should be confined solely to the anal area and then rinsed off immediately.

Another enormous temptation for women suffering from recurrent urinary tract infections or vaginitis is to antisepticize the erring organs. The more severe the trouble, the more likely women are to use cotton swabs containing undiluted antiseptic. Unbearable stinging and burning usually start immediately, but some martyrs will stand this pain, thinking it must be doing some good if it hurts so much! Within hours the genital organs are massively swollen and inflamed; in a few cases it may even be difficult for urine to flow out of the swollen urethra. Diluted antiseptics over a short period of time will bring about intense pubic irritation and small boils. One woman with exactly this condition, incidentally one that was totally mysterious to her doctor, was swabbing her perineum with antiseptic, washing her panties in it, and wiping the toilet seat with neat antiseptic before sitting down. She was weeping in agony before she was finally straightened out.

Never use antiseptic on your bottom—*never!*

So you can see the point in being careful about soaps and antiseptics. "Well, talcum powders are surely safe." Not at all! Their fine particles probe every nook and cranny of your perineum. Irritation will set in very quickly, and because talcum powder is such an everyday household product, the thought of its actually being capable of provoking an attack of cystitis seems out of the question. Ask yourself, among many other questions, whether the current attack can be traced to your starting to use a new talcum powder or any new toiletry.

Creams! "If it irritates, I smooth on some anti-itch cream; but it lasts only a few minutes, and then it gets bad again!"

Of course it does. A perineum is ten times more sensitive than any other part of the body and reacts badly to foreign invasion. Creams and lotions prescribed by doctors are often just as bad, and if irritation or stinging increases under a prescribed cream, stop it immediately, and pour cool water down the perineum to remove the substance.

Sometimes bowel or anal conditions like hemorrhoids need suppositories and creams. Use them sparingly, and try to confine them to the anal region, using a small piece of lint or cotton. Swab the urethral and vaginal openings more often with plain warm water front to back to keep them free of contamination.

Don't be tempted to try the anti-itch cream in a newspaper ad. There is no substitute at all for finding the basic reason for your itch. Only when this is discovered and treated will the irritation disappear.

The last three or four years have seen a new and insidious addition to female hygiene requirements: antiseptic cleansing tissues. It really begins to look in a drugstore as though the town's water supply has ceased to exist and that extraneous aids to hygiene have had to be designed to replace it! Your bottom doesn't need expensive cleansing tissues; it prefers cheap ordinary water. Toilet paper has never really been documented as causing cystitis, though some women feel the dyes may be a contributory factor. Safety is assured by using soft white tissue with a dabbing rather than rubbing movement.

Never abandon the excellent washing procedures herein detailed, and never use chemical hygiene aids.

Correct laundering of underwear is important. Many of the common irritations can be induced by the use of strong biological washing powders. There appears to be a buildup process on the skin, and certainly it is clearly possible to see what happens to hands in contact with such chemicals. The same dryness and irritation could be happening to the perineum as well. Since cystitis and vaginitis patients must always wear cotton pants, these can be safely boiled after use, with perhaps a small addition of soap powder now and then to brighten them. Women should own seven or eight pairs and never wear the same pair next day. They may look clean, but they have plenty of unseen bacteria all over the crotch.

Don't use the launderette for washing underwear. Biological washing powders leave deposits around the machines, and this will infiltrate your underwear.

Many women experience frequency; they just want to keep on visiting the toilet. All medical investigations are negative, but there's no relief of the trouble. Usually such women, on interrogation, will admit to including their panties in the weekly wash at the launderette. This chemically contaminates them either right away or over several weeks. The chemical builds up in turn on the urethral and vaginal orifices, irritating the skin. Boiling panties in plain water will stop frequency in large numbers of women.

Tampons or sanitary pads? If these are causing trouble, their use occurs over such a short time span that isolating them as a cause of vaginitis or cystitis is relatively easy. Tampons and applicators need plenty of KY jelly to aid insertion, and then the patient has to bear in mind possible trouble spots.

A tampon is:

1. Drying
2. Chemically treated in order to keep its compressed shape
3. Capable of sustaining bacteria on the string
4. Easy to forget toward the end of menstruation.

There is a terrifying story of a manicurist in a fashionable hairdresser's who developed a vicious attack of cystitis out of the blue. She was treated with antibiotics and remained in bed for three weeks. Tracing what may have caused it led her back to her first-ever use of tampons. She found them dry and awkward to insert, so she felt that a lubricant would help. She used cuticle-remover cream and nearly removed her vagina in the bargain!

Sanitary pads are the only alternative, unless you make your own and boil them as great-grand-mama did. Go for a product of an old and trusted name, and there should be no complications.

This short chapter on chemical contamination cannot take into account all the individually strange things that women do to themselves. It has, I hope, convinced you that the products you use in good faith on your bottom are all unnecessary and all potentially dangerous.

Do not use any other way of cleansing yourself than directed in this book, and do not seek to reduce your troubles with chemical products.

14. Settling Down

Carrying a child for nine months indisputably marks the end of mental and physical freedom for women everywhere. The first sacrifice on offer is your own health. Sometimes this is only temporary, but often there is a lifelong effect, for no woman comes out of pregnancy and childbirth completely unmarked. The process of birth, if you are lucky, can be a memorable experience for many years; but like all things, it recedes into fog as the years go by, and often even the birth dates of children become difficult to recall on request.

By looking at their bodies and by knowing the impediments brought on through procreation, women are daily reminded that they have indeed made their first real sacrifice. It is unfortunately unavoidable. Something or someone has to ensure the future generation. Perhaps it may be machines one day, as in the manner of the first experiments in growing test-tube babies, or there may be a good "bank" of host mothers for whom childbirth is as easy as antelopes dropping their young in the veldt. Then those women who do not wish to risk their health either experimentally or with real reasons may in peace of mind transfer their "happy burden" and remain wholesome.

Women in general have only one real problem. It is their uterus. As long as women have uteri, they cannot be independent, they cannot live without social regard as men do, and they cannot be in the peak of health every day. Men do not understand what it is like to feel inwardly tired unless they are working eighteen hours a day or are extremely ill. Men do not understand the mental and physical urgency of growing a child inside them. But to increasing numbers of women with widening horizons and monetary status the prospect of motherhood seems like slavery. (In fact, it is, but mother love is the antidote, the one component of the slavery that makes it bearable, indeed, for many very pleasurable.) Historical reasons for large families—unpaid labor by the offspring, financial assistance from them in the parents' old age, high infant mortality which required many births to assure some of the children's survival—are largely obsolete today except in the Third World. With better pay, good contraceptives, and life-giving drugs, reductions in the number of each family's children are seen to be occurring.

Mother's health is much improved, and she begins to be available for sexual pleasure rather than procreation. But just one pregnancy and one resulting baby can take its physical toll of the mother's body, and centuries ago this was well recognized. When the marriage service was devised with its accent on "forsaking all others until death do us part," death was maybe only nine months or multiples of nine away. Few women lived long enough to plague their husbands, who, in any case, frequently sought sexual gratification elsewhere. Childbirth was very dangerous, and marriages were frequently arranged with brides who had strong bones, healthy dispositions, and good childbearing hips.

Childbirth is still basically as dangerous as it was, but now that our doctors have overcome most of the problems, maternal mortality is rare. Much mental disturbance was overcome in olden times by the presence of mothers, sisters, or good friends at the lying-in. Today this is seldom allowed unless home delivery is strongly requested and medically approved.

With the second confinement one is experienced. It is the first baby that proves such a petrifying experience, surrounded as we are by shift doctors and temporary nurses.

Impersonal directions from strangers, mountains of machinery, fear of behaving badly, and fear of the unknown are what modern first-time mothers face in hospitals. In family confinements there must have been plenty of childbirth chat to take one's mind off things and give one confidence, plenty of advice good and bad to think about, and soothing hands to hold.

Despite all the books on the subject, first-time experience is all too frequently hard. Girls often have no older confidantes these days—mother, aunt, and granny live too far away and in truth really are worlds away from what girls of today think, feel, and practice.

Only in the last few years has it been possible for a young woman to live openly with the man of her choice. Marriage was the only way for women of all classes to have regular sex, and one braved society's reactions if one stepped out of line.

This kind of revolutionary behavior might appear to be following on with a second, because women are choosing not only whether or not to have a baby this year but whether or not to have any at all. The birthrate in Sweden has fallen well below the death rate, and it can only be a short time before other countries follow suit. Should women refusing to have children be considered selfish, or are many other women secretly, very secretly, jealous?

How many young women hear older ones ask, "Was it worth it?" Was it really worth the sacrifice of bearing and rearing children to have them not only leave home but leave the area or even the country? If old people who have had children are lonely and unwanted, what difference then is there if one never has any in the first place?

There is a saying that children keep one young, but that is only in thought. Ask any woman if she feels that her prechildbirth vitality has fully returned, and she will answer that she doesn't think it has. After a year or so she forgets, of course, and thinks she is normally active.

During pregnancy a woman becomes acutely sensitive to herself. She recognizes the primevalness of her existence and submits, since instinct and choice have persuaded her to. For the first time she vomits without any stomach virus causing such discomfort. It is a strange, uncontrollable vomit, causing some misery for part or all of the next nine months, and she learns which food and drink exacerbate these horrid sessions.

Early on she realizes that she is excreting a lot more urine and tires by 9:00 P.M., whereas she used to be lively at 11:00. Sexual intercourse becomes genteel in an instinctive effort to protect the fetus.

Perhaps this fact plus the extra urine is sufficient to stop attacks of cystitis in many pregnant women. Maybe it is the extra hormone circulating through all areas of the body, including the urethra and bladder, which is responsible, or maybe the body automatically becomes more resistant to all infections. The scientific speculation on this phenomenon of recurrent cystitis patients is not as readily apparent as it should be, but this certainly is a fact: Patients suffering from recurrent cystitis often have no attacks at all during pregnancy.

The medical profession tends to look thoughtfully only at those women who *commence* cystitis during pregnancy. Then discussion and therapy center on the best sort of antibiotic to use. Obviously the health of the unborn child is important, but since urinary infections tend to occur from the fifth month onward, administering drugs is regarded seriously.

The theory on urinary infection during later pregnancy is that hormone action in the kidneys slows up the production of urine, and the growing baby impedes the flow of urine.

Not all freshly manufactured urine is excreted within its normal time, and with the slower flow out of the urethra quite a lot remains to become stale. Stale urine harbors germs, and this very often causes infection in later pregnancy.

There is a way of ensuring that as much urine as possible is passed each time you visit the bathroom. It is especially good for pregnant women, handicapped people, and old people and is known as double emptying.

In such cases a lot of effort is required in the

first place to get the handicapped and elderly onto
the toilet. It makes sense to squeeze as much urine
as possible out of their bladders so that the great
performance does not have to be repeated half an
hour later.

In double emptying, toward the end of the flow
the patient stops, consciously pulls up all the muscles around the perineum, then bends over and releases the muscles, pushing as well to help expel
more urine. If quite a lot comes away, stop again
and repeat. Pull up the muscles; bend over; then release and push.

In pregnancy, particularly in the last month,
this process can be repeated until no urine escapes
at all.

So it is:

1. Pull up.
2. Bend over.
3. Push down.

All the washing rules apply, and if the patient is
prone to cystitis in the later months, the perineum
can be cleansed after each passing of urine.

This extra washing will help the anus. Most
women during the last month or so of pregnancy
have bowel problems. Hemorrhoids (piles) are
caused by the constant downward pressure of the
growing fetus and marked further by the daily
opening of the bowels. This habit usually alters in
pregnancy, and often women need a gentle laxative.
Piles will be worse if a good stool is not passed each
day. The weight of the stools inside adds to the
weight of the baby, and the delicate veins and bowel
linings become engorged. There is nothing to prevent this except ensuring that bowels are regularly
cleared out and that weight is taken off the lower

abdomen as much as possible. Plenty of cold-water compresses to the anus will help keep the swelling down a little, but antihemorrhoidal creams and suppositories are also frequently used.

Piles, particularly external piles, are carriers of *E. coli* contamination and therefore necessitate strict and fairly frequent washing. This will lessen the risk of urinary infection.

Sex during pregnancy should not be deeply penetrating. A barrage of penile thrusts on the cervix will not only bruise it but also possibly disturb the baby. The safest entries are those most comfortable, and the husband should be slow in movements, using thoughts rather than deeds to encourage ejaculation.

Having cystitis regularly before becoming pregnant is not a barrier to conception except when hormones are a major factor in causing your attacks. The ovaries and uterus function regardless of whether your renal organs are coping with troubles. What you must realize, though, is that the demands of a baby are never-ending. Can you still get through an attack? The chances of your cystitis continuing after birth are the same as they always have been, until you or your doctor find the cause.

Throughout the first and second stages of labor the patient loses a lot of fluid. Not only are her waters coming away, but her bladder seems to be making up for the decrease in urine output over the last three months. Whether you ask for the bedpan or commode or whether the nurse puts you on one at regular intervals makes no difference; you will fill it each time! No replacement liquid is given, and no replacement is necessary since you are like a camel living off its storage. Only ice cubes to suck or a sponge or minute sips of water are allowed, and when the end of the second stage is reached, minutes before the head emerges, the midwife or doctor may decide to catheterize. A small plastic tube is inserted up the urethra into the bladder to allow a clear passage for trapped bladder urine. When this comes out, the baby has less to fight and will come down the vagina a little more easily.

An episiotomy is a recent addition to labor performed perhaps too frequently these days. In times past mothers were left to push and strain sometimes for hours in the final stage of labor. The effect on the body was to stretch practically everything in the abdomen beyond the point where it might revert eventually back to its original position. Prolapsed (out-of-place) uterus was common in most women who had borne a child, and the more you had, the worse your own health became. Women in poorer areas and with short recovery times walked around with their vaginas and cervixes actually visible and hanging out!

Since anesthetics facilitated stitches, such appalling maternity care has improved. Although now and again care of the mother's vagina after birth is not up to standard, the majority of women do experience repair work. The episiotomy is usually performed by the doctor while the patient is on the crest of a powerful contraction. If you have been pushing with little or no reward and the perineum is stretched unbearably, this slit from the vagina toward the anus is performed, and the baby's head comes through more easily. Without this help many mothers have finally torn, and it is more difficult to sew up jagged edges than a straight line.

Episiotomy, helpful as it may have been in facilitating birth, is often a source of trouble in the years to come. It can open at weak points like a newspaper fold which becomes worn. It can be affected every time the patient has intercourse or passes a hard stool, becoming sore and splitting. Surgical repair work has to be undertaken when it reaches a pitch of exasperation, but the patient has to understand that scar tissue, particularly here, is extremely tender and needs much patience. Women need doctors who are better able to judge when episiotomy is necessary, not men who shorten labor time to suit their own commitments.

Yet another point of prospective urinary troubles which women are often incapable of protesting about at the time is the insensitive use of strong antiseptics after delivery. Since antiseptics were discovered to be capable of reducing infection, one of the first areas of health in which they were used was after delivery. A wash-down of the perineum at this time has to be done, but surely cool water with a tiny amount of antiseptic should be sufficient.

Hexachlorophene solutions are still present for swabbing down in operating rooms, although stringent rules have been laid down by government health regulations. This so-called antiseptic has been the subject of much discussion over recent years, and its use in baby products and adult cosmetics has been either banned or severely curtailed. On a raw, bleeding, swollen, and very painful newly delivered mother's perineum this sort of thoughtlessness just adds to her discomfort. All the patient can do is beg the nurse or midwife to use a very mild antiseptic, well diluted because of possible urinary sensitivity.

When the new mother is back in her room, recovery of the bruised and split skin will be helped a lot by air. Unfortunately, pads must be worn for several days while the uterus is healing and drying out.

Large but thin maternity pads are provided by the patient or by the hospital, and so long as one is placed well to the back to catch backward-flowing drainage, the front part can be relaxed. A loose pair of cotton panties with plenty of air routes would be helpful. So will long, not short, cotton nighties because then you can throw the bedclothes back, bend the legs up, and still present a modest frontage. Plenty of air can then circulate between your legs to heal your skin. In America (although not in England) some doctors use an ultraviolet light to aid tissue-healing processes.

The more you rest with your legs up, the better will be your recovery, and for several months, or as long as you need, you should snatch an occasional hour to take the weight off your bottom.

Some six to eight weeks later you may commence intercourse. Be free with the KY jelly, and don't hesitate to guide your partner's penis slowly. Sexual intercourse after childbirth is often uncomfortable, to say the least. Circles or lengths of painful sensitivity will reveal themselves when penile contact upsets the new scars or tired muscles. Lubrication and gentle perseverance with lots of cold water afterward and plenty of time between each session are essential. Even a year or more later if delivery was particularly difficult, intercourse may still be painful. The pain should go away eventually, and you will know if it is subsiding a little month by month. Obviously unbearable vaginal or cervical pain each time you have intercourse must be investigated—perhaps the doctor left his needle up there!

Fortunately the vagina, despite its acute sensitivity, is elastic and, as such, pretty strong. It can put up with a lot and still come out all right.

To strengthen it after delivery and to help the pelvis go back to shape, you may have the good fortune to be visited by a physiotherapist. She should visit your bed each day to take you through some exercises. Such exercises are gentle and reassuring; also, they are done in bed, taking the hard work out of it. Each physiotherapist has her own set of exercises, but here are five.

Lie comfortably flat on the cover of your bed with just one slim pillow under your head. Lie still, and concentrate on your body. Remind yourself of what you own—toes, feet, heels, ankles, calves, knees, thighs, perineum, abdomen, waist, ribs, chest, fingers, wrists, elbows, arms, shoulders, neck, jaw, cheeks, eyes, head. Now think back to below waist level and begin:

1. Breathe deeply so that your abdomen below the waist rises up to a count of slow one, two, three; then let the breath out, and pull your abdomen hard down as flat as it will go and hold it again on a count of slow one, two, three.

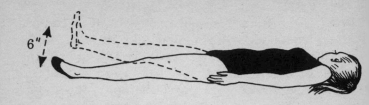

2. Still lying flat, think of your feet. One at a time point the toes skyward so that your foot is straight, and stiffen it. Slowly, to a count of six, lift the foot approximately six inches off the bed, and lower it again to a count of six. Don't lift it higher off the bed because the resulting perineal muscular contraction might be lost. Alternate the legs, and repeat the exercise twice.

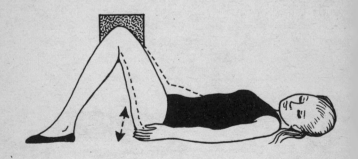

3. Still lying flat, pull up the knees, and put a thin hardback book between them so that the knees clutch the book. Push your waist into the bed, and let your bottom rise off the bed to a slow count of three. Maintain this for one count, and again pull the abdomen down to meet the waist. When it is as tight down as you can manage, lower the bottom and relax. Repeat the process three times.

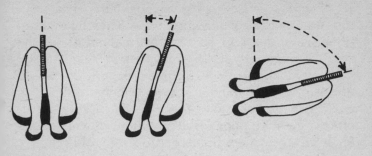

4. Still lying flat and clutching the book with your knees, do the knee sway. Think of a clock face. You are now at 12:00. On sway one go to five minutes past and back to 12:00. On sway two go to ten minutes past and back to 12:00. On the quarter past your knees should touch the bed. Do the exercise first to the right and then to the left. It will soon show how weak or strong your pelvic floor is.

5. Last one! Lie flat with the legs down and the feet pointing up to the ceiling. From the waist down stiffen everything—feet, legs, abdomen, perineum, and waist. Hold it for a count of eight, and daily add more counts so that you can almost hold it indefinitely while you breathe lightly underneath the rib cage.

These exercises are good for your pelvis at all times, not just after having a baby. They take ten to fifteen minutes and require no real effort. Doing them throughout your life may help you avoid a sagging stomach, stress incontinence, and prolapsed uterus, troubles which are miserable and difficult to treat. A bad prolapsed uterus needs surgery and is often done with poor results. Millions of women suffer from stress incontinence as they get older.

Coughing, sneezing, laughing, or any jerking movement can make a weakened, aging bladder valve open involuntarily and allow urine out. This is not only embarrassing but very depressing, so caring for your pelvic health can pay dividends in later years.

Hormone replacement therapy is not self-help, but since it involves the happiness and well-being of countless women, it must be mentioned. Life expectancy for centuries took women only into their forties or fifties. Only a minority came to know and understand the menopause, and they simply used to put up with it, becoming reclusive to conceal their poor health.

Hysterectomy, removal of the uterus and/or ovaries, belongs to twentieth-century medicine and has increased in incidence.

If cystitis attacks or burning urine have occurred at menopause or after a hysterectomy the patient should insist on a referral to a hormone therapy clinic, which is usually integrated within gynecology units. There experts will assess the state of the vagina, which is usually dry in such cases, and decide whether a course of hormone treatment would improve matters. If they do decide to prescribe something, they will grade the treatment to suit your needs.

Maybe use of the mildest vaginal cream for only six weeks is all that is needed. At the other extreme tablets taken for many months might be prescribed. In between come varying dosages of different pills and creams. It is essentially up to the patient to describe her progress at the two or three monthly consultations. It will come right eventually, and you can always ask for a second opinion if time and one doctor don't produce results.

Hormone treatment for old women with recurrent urinary trouble is very successful and well documented, but patients don't have to be old to require hormone help. Doctors think nothing of prescribing the Pill for contraception or menorrhagia (severe menstrual distress), and since it is safely and widely used for those purposes, it should be possible to prescribe if hormone imbalance is diagnosed and coincides with the onset of other difficulties including cystitis—i.e., teenage, after a baby when all other possibilities are eliminated, menopause, and hysterectomy.

Hormone imbalance is a fashionable subject. That is why help should only be sought from a hormone therapy clinic or a good gynecologist. Haphazard hormones are as stupid as haphazard antibiotics.

Take care of your perineum all through your life. It wears out just like other parts of you, but somehow it causes much more physical and mental distress when it is ill.

15. Oddments

Many women feel very alone with their urinary troubles because they do not chat openly with other sufferers and fail to realize the wide extent of this kind of trouble. Perhaps in a way that is good, for medically ignorant women could do great harm to one another in comparing symptoms and trying out identical managements. It is safer to read quietly to oneself and glean information which would be appropriate to you rather than try what "Mrs. Smith" did.

If you have read this far, you've probably inferred that there are as many causes for urinary/vaginal ailments as there are types of houses. Nonetheless, it is very comforting to find your particular idea or cause given a mention.

Here are some extra thoughts, some slightly odder connections, if you like, with urinary troubles. None is probed deeply since most of them are only for medical treatment. All have at some time been mentioned more than once to the author, though in some cases it might have been only twice!

Female sterilization is being used more often

these days as a permanent method of birth control. Cases of pelvic congestion are occurring but this information is not always relayed to a prospective patient to help her decide. It is thought that normal body liquids reach the "dead end" of the looped or tied tubes and can go no farther. Bacteria could be harbored and pelvic infection result.

In vasectomy, congestion of one or both testicles may arise on the first intercourse after a gap of a few weeks. The first ejaculation eases it, and thereafter there are no further sensations. For the wife the changed content of her husband's seminal fluid may feel a little different, perhaps too acid, but with the normal sexual hygiene routines this is absolutely no problem.

Smelly urine with lethargy, dizziness, dry tongue, thirst, and temperature usually means a toxemic state, an overall blood-borne infection. Antibiotic therapy is indicated.

Active sports on a regular weekly basis may be doing odd things to a sensitive bladder or vagina. Sports often mean contact with a variety of bacteria in public dressing rooms and toilets. If your bladder symptoms arise in the vicinity of your regular sports outing, check any suspect routine.

You may be in the wrong job! Sitting from nine to five on the edge of a hard chair or one with a man-made fiber covering can cause vaginitis, soreness, or frequency. Sit back on chairs to reduce urethral pressure, and make sure that chemically contaminated panties aren't contaminating the urethra and vagina. Any job that restricts visits to the toilet or ease of drinking may be troublesome. Escorts or guides get very little chance to sit, drink, or visit the bathroom. If you're a prostitute, well, good luck to you; there are many housewives unable to have a faintly reasonable sex life with one man, let alone four or more different ones every night!

A few women have allied their cystitis to a smear test (Pap test), and the reason could be rough handling or introduction of infection.

A gallbladder-removal operation has also been pinpointed as a starting point for cystitis by more than one woman.

Part of all check questions when the doctor is trying to diagnose the cause of a patient's cystitis should be: "Have you ever injured your back?" It could be as simple as sitting down hard or as complicated as being involved in a road crash. If all other tests prove negative, a neurological survey should be undertaken. Bladder nerve impulses can be disturbed by a neurological injury, however small.

Sinusitis, conjunctivitis, tracheitis can be combined with bladder troubles in all sorts of ways—i.e., blood-borne infection from a draining pus-filled sinus passing through the kidneys, making urine become smelly and later infected as well. If the sinus bacteria match the urinary bacteria, you have a cause for that particular kind of cystitis. Swabs are highly important.

Frequent dilatations, except where interstitial cystitis is indicated, should be fought. They will not prevent infections or improve the functioning of the urethra, which may only in recent months have begun to let you down. If you spent a comfortable childhood, adolescence, or young adulthood, there is no change in the good physical working of your urethra, so why let some strange doctor convince you otherwise? Get a second opinion.

Stress, whether of the short, sharp kind or the

long, insidious, draining variety, eventually becomes something physical. All sorts of illnesses (such as headaches and limb pains) are stress-induced. Women in concentration camps frequently stopped menstruating. Put a woman in her forties as nurse to a very close relative dying of terminal cancer, and she will bear up well but probably to the detriment of her hormone balance. The imbalance worsens until it shows up first as a dry vagina, but it can go quickly on to greater vaginal and urethral troubles. Excitement stress, such as that an actress faces on opening night, will increase the kidney output of urine, and the actress will have to visit the toilet quite a lot before her appearance.

A car accident will find victims either vomiting or urinating—this is a stress reaction. The bladder functions differently from normal under stress.

Bladder cancer is not common in women. It is more so in men, but with modern cauterization the tumors can be kept small. A general anesthetic and cautery every three to four months can usually prolong life until old age arrives. Bladder cancer is to be found more in heavy smokers as a rule, and any involuntary, painless bleeding from the male urethra should be quickly examined.

For stubborn sexual cystitis that has failed to respond as favorably as the vast majority of cases do to self-help rules, one antibiotic capsule or one sulfonamide tablet either before or after intercourse can act preventively. Even a urinary antiseptic can just be enough to give a little extra push to awkward germs. Experiment (under your doctor's guidance) one at a time, and see which is best suited to you, but only after you have conducted the exhaustive measures for self-help contained herein.

A strong hymen (virginity) and narrow fibrous vaginal orifices can cause horrible sexual tensions. If your sexual partner or previous partners have failed to penetrate your vagina, you must seek medical help. At least one woman has spent thirty years of marriage in a separate bedroom because her hymen was too thick and she was easily embarrassed. Surgically, the hymen is easy to deal with, but a taut small orifice demands careful specialized surgery. Any old gynecologist won't do. Techniques of skill are involved because if loose pieces of vagina are left to flap around, they will tear or become infected each time intercourse takes place.

Medical help is expensive everywhere. In countries with some kind of national health or national medical insurance plan, help is obviously available although not always willing to slog away at difficult cases. Therefore, wherever you live, it makes sound sense to have private medical insurance. Use it for second opinions or use it for only one illness—that preferably starting after you joined the plan—or use it more broadly any time real trouble starts.

Women who have no possible sexual reason for their cystitis because they are not having intercourse still have all the other hundreds of causes to explore together with their medical advisers. Monks and nuns are no strangers to bladder and vaginal troubles.

Arthritis related to cystitis or vice versa is one of the symptoms of Reiter's disease. This is a sexually transmitted disease joining hands with nonspecific urethritis—sort of like a genealogy table with third cousins twice removed by marriage! A venereologist is perhaps the best person to help.

Over the past five years many doctors have begun to recommend a daily intake of bran for patients suffering from diverticulitis or constipation. Bran contains about 20 percent of indigestible cellulose, which, by being bulky and stimulating the walls of the bowel, produces feces that are relatively easy to pass. Bran is a derivative of wheat. Wheat is an extremely common allergic substance. In many people it produces reactions like a runny nose or wheezing. Too many people other than those with bowel disorders now follow advice from well-meaning doctors and health food stores by liberally sprinkling meals with bran. Many of these men and women have mysterious frequency of urination as a result. They trek from doctor to doctor, and no one ever dreams that the cause of their frequency is bran. If you suffer from frequency or unexplained bladder tingling, cut out the bran for two weeks, and see whether your bladder problem resolves itself. The allergic properties of bran, in being ejected as waste products within urine, will irritate and aggravate the bladder lining, making you want to pass urine frequently.

Cows eat grass and hay. Their milk and cream contains nutrients from that grass. Some people are allergic to milk, which can result in unexplained continuous minor health troubles like skin rashes, sinusitis, frequency. Are you allergic to grass, milk, wheat, or bran? Omit these items or anything else suspicious from your diet for two weeks, and see if you get better.

Doctors, when they deliberate on female cystitis, have a favorite *question formidable:* "Why do some women get it and some not?"

Indeed, why not? What makes one-half of female humanity less likely to have attacks of cystitis?

Theorizing ends up on one of two roads. First, so far hormone imbalance is under discussion in the occasional, really enlightened research programs. It is still rare to see an article on hormone imbalance in women *under* fifty years, let alone one specifying a link with cystitis. At least it is a case of "rare" rather than "never." The second road of theorizing is skin sensitivity or cell sensitivity. If some skins throw off an invasion of bacteria, does the same rejection occur in the rest or have these not such well-developed antitoxins (infection resistants)? To the author's current knowledge no research or discussion takes place on this quite simple reasoning with respect to cystitis.

Every symposium on urinary tract problems in which the author has taken part included a bacteriologist, who lectures on germs; a urologist or general surgeon, who lectures on renal causes of cystitis; and perhaps a gynecologist or venereologist. No organizer has ever departed from this ordered form and thrown provocative speakers at his usually sleepy audience of medical personnel. It would be nice to make an endocrinologist or dermatologist exercise his mind to see if hormones and skin do play a big role in urinary troubles.

True, pioneer medicine sometimes necessitates clutching at straws. Hold the straw, dissect it, and then understand it. It may bring hitherto-unknown rewards, and certainly recurrent cystitis demands just that. I wrote this book to help you solve your cystitis problem. Help yourself!

Glossary of Terms

Analgesic	A pain-relieving substance
Antibiotic	Substance produced by a microorganism to inhibit growth of or kill another microorganism such as a disease germ
Anus	Opening at the end of alimentary canal for passage of feces
Bacteria	Microscopic plants that can cause disease
Bicarbonate of soda	Baking soda; alkalinizing agent
Bladder, urinary	Elastic sac in the pelvic region for urine storage
Candida	Genus of fungi that cause vaginal inflammation
Candidiasis	Infection caused by *Candida*
Catheterization	Insertion of catheter (small tube) into an organ; used to withdraw urine from urinary bladder

Cauterization — Burning away of abnormal or injured tissue

Cautery — Synonym for cauterization; the agent used to cauterize

Cervicitis — Any inflammation of the cervix

Cervix — Narrow lower or outer end of the womb

Colitis — Inflammation of the colon

Cryosurgery — Operation in which extreme cold produces desired dissection

Cystitis — Inflammation of the urinary bladder

Cystoscopy — Surgical procedure for the visual examination of the bladder

Diabetes — Disorders marked by excessive excretion of urine, especially diabetes mellitus, in which there is inadequate secretion of insulin

Dialysis — Chemical process that is used in artificial kidney machine to purify blood of persons suffering from kidney malfunction

Dilatation — Enlargement of cervix or urethra by insertion of rods

Diuretic — An agent which stimulates the production of urine

Diverticulitis — Inflammation of diverticulum, an abnormal sac opening from a bodily organ such as the intestines. Diverticulums may also be found in the bladder.

E. coli Bacteria found in the intestines which may cause disease elsewhere

Episiotomy Operation on perineum during difficult childbirth

Epithelium Tissue that covers free surface or lines tubes or cavities of the body

Estrogen Female sex hormone

Foreskin Fold of skin that covers the glans of penis

Fungus Parasitic plant that may produce infection

Hematuria Presence of blood in the urine

Herpes One of several inflammatory viral skin diseases marked by clusters of watery blisters

Hormone Substance carried from a gland or body organ by the bloodstream to effect a particular activity

Hysterectomy Surgical removal of the uterus

Ileostomy Surgery to create artificial excretory process

Interstitial cystitis Degenerative disease of the bladder lining

IVP Intravenous pyelogram; kidney X rays

Labia (majora/minora) Folds of skin which protect vaginal orifices

Leukorrhea Discharge from the vagina resulting from excessive cell rejection

Litmus paper	Chemical paper used to test for acidity and alkalinity
Menopause	Natural process involving termination of menstruation
Micturating cystogram	An X ray taken during urination
Micturition	Act of urinating
Monilia	Genus of fungi that cause vaginal inflammation
Moniliasis	Infection caused by *Monilia*
Nephropexy	Surgical fixation of floating kidney
NSU	Nonspecific urethritis
Orifice	Opening
Ovulation	Release of unfertilized egg from ovaries
Perineum	Base of body's trunk containing excretal organs
Potassium citrate	Alkalinizing agent
Proctologist	Doctor specializing in diseases of the rectum and bowels
Prolapsed uterus	Dropped womb
Prostatectomy	Surgical removal of the prostate gland
Prostate gland	Male sex gland through which urethra passes
Prostasis	Inflammation of the prostate gland
Pyelitis	Inflammation of the lining of the pelvis or a kidney
Pyelogram	X ray of the kidney
Radiographer	Specialist in X ray techniques

Rectum	Terminal part of the intestines
Reflux	Flow in the wrong direction
Streptococcus	A form of bacteria
Thrush	Vaginal yeast infection, also called candidiasis or moniliasis
Trichomonas	Genus of parasitic protozoans
Trichomoniasis	Vaginal infection caused by *Trichomonas*
Ureters	Tubes carrying urine from the kidneys
Urethra	Tube carrying urine from urinary bladder
Urethritis	Inflammation of the urethra
Uric acid	Acid excreted by kidneys and present in urine
Urologist	Doctor specializing in renal organs
Uterus	Womb
UTI	Urinary tract infection
Vagina	Canal from the uterus to the vulva
Vaginitis	Any inflammation of the vagina
Yeast	Yellowish, frothy substance containing fungus cells. Also called candidiasis, moniliasis or thrush

Index